THE VISUAL DICTIONARY *of* EVERYDAY THINGS

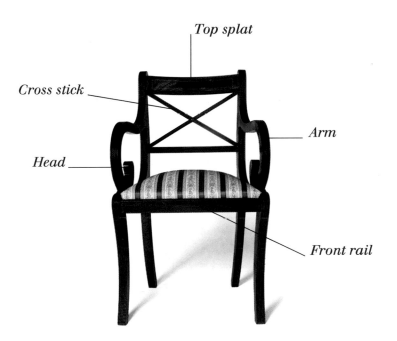

Top splat

Cross stick

Arm

Head

Front rail

FRONT VIEW OF CHAIR

Intermediate ring

Reel seat

Screw locking nut

Tip ring

Butt cap

Hand grip

FLY ROD

Escape wheel

Cradle switch

Earpiece

Hub

Pinion

Spoke

Third wheel

Base

Handset

Rim

Center wheel

INTERNAL WORKINGS OF CLOCK

Inner tube

Winding key

**EXTERNAL VIEW
OF TELEPHONE**

Tongue

Cuff

Valve

Vamp

Counter

Wing cap

GRENSON
6154/19 7/EX

Outsole

CROSS SECTION OF FINISHED SHOE

Heel

Tire

FRONT WHEEL

THE VISUAL
DICTIONARY *of*
EVERYDAY
THINGS

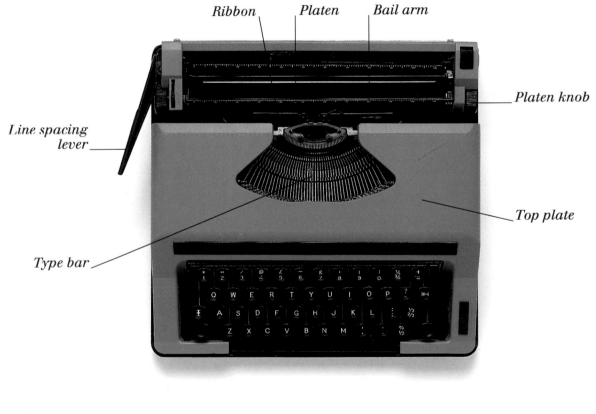

Ribbon   Platen   Bail arm

Platen knob

Line spacing
lever

Top plate

Type bar

EXTERNAL VIEW OF TYPEWRITER

DORLING KINDERSLEY
LONDON • NEW YORK • STUTTGART

A DORLING KINDERSLEY BOOK

PROJECT ART EDITOR ROSS GEORGE
DESIGNER JOHNNY PAU
DESIGN ASSISTANT LESLEY BETTS

PROJECT EDITORS TIM FRASER, STEPHANIE JACKSON, PAUL DOCHERTY
RESEARCHER CLIVE WEBSTER

SERIES ART EDITOR PAUL WILKINSON
ART DIRECTOR CHEZ PICTHALL
MANAGING EDITOR RUTH MIDGLEY

PHOTOGRAPHY DAVE KING, STEVE GORTON, TIM RIDLEY

PRODUCTION HILARY STEPHENS

Front hackle

Tail

Head

Wing

DEER HOPPER DRY FLY

FIRST AMERICAN EDITION, 1991

10 9 8 7 6 5 4 3 2 1

DORLING KINDERSLEY, INC., 232 MADISON AVENUE
NEW YORK, NEW YORK 10016

ISBN: 1-879431-17-3 (TRADE EDITION)
ISBN: 1-879431-32-7 (LIBRARY EDITION)

LIBRARY OF CONGRESS CARD CATALOG NUMBER: 91-060898

REPRODUCED BY GRB GRAFICA, VERONA, ITALY
PRINTED AND BOUND BY ARNOLDO MONDADORI, VERONA, ITALY

Contents

Lapel

Pocket flap

Wedge pleat lining

TRENCH COAT

Rewind belt

Playback head

Auto-stop lever

CHASSIS ASSEMBLY OF PERSONAL STEREO

Saddle

Fork blade

Arm

Screw hole

Bearing

GEARCASE OF POWER DRILL

Counter stiffener

Back lining

Counter

HEEL UPPERS

Band

Handle

Canopy

AUTOMATIC COLLAPSIBLE UMBRELLA

CLOCK 6

SUIT 8

TELEPHONE 10

PENCILS AND PENS 12

PERSONAL STEREO 14

BATTERIES 16

FISHING ROD 18

DRILLS 20

SHOES 22

SHAVERS AND RAZORS 24

BOOKS 26

CAMERA 28

TEDDY BEAR 30

LAMP 32

CHAINSAW 34

MINI TELEVISION 36

CHAIR 38

FOOD PROCESSOR 40

TYPEWRITER 42

SUITCASE 44

TOASTER 46

UMBRELLAS 48

LAWNMOWER 50

SADDLE 52

ESPRESSO MACHINE 54

TRENCH COAT 56

BICYCLE 58

INDEX 60

ACKNOWLEDGMENTS 64

Clock

MECHANICAL CLOCKS HAVE TWO essential elements: a mainspring and a pendulum. When the clock is wound with the key, the mainspring is tightened. As the mainspring unwinds, it turns the gears, which move the minute and hour hands at different speeds around the face of the clock. The pendulum ensures that the hands move at a regular pace. At the top of the pendulum are two hooks called pallets. As the pendulum swings, the pallets allow the escape wheel to turn slowly and evenly.

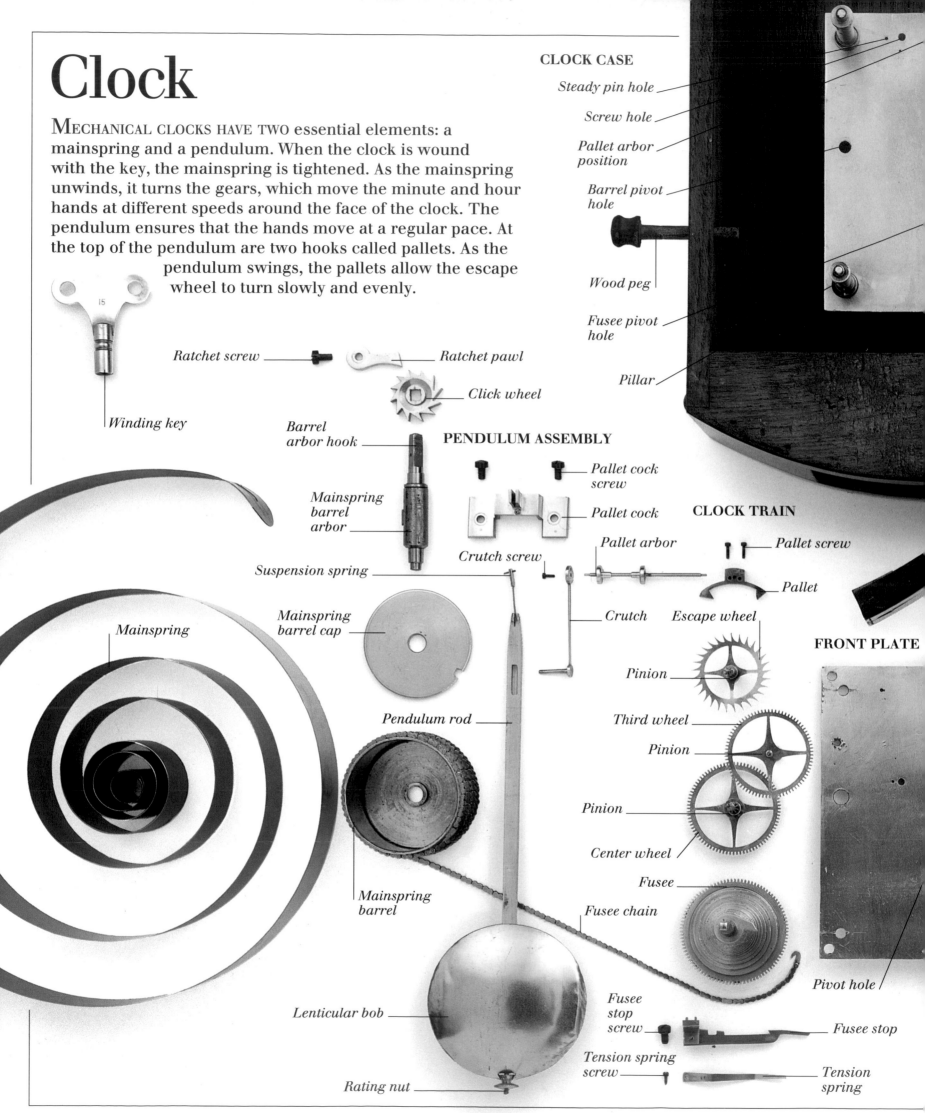

CLOCK CASE

Steady pin hole

Screw hole

Pallet arbor position

Barrel pivot hole

Wood peg

Fusee pivot hole

Pillar

Ratchet screw

Winding key

Ratchet pawl

Click wheel

Barrel arbor hook

PENDULUM ASSEMBLY

Mainspring barrel arbor

Pallet cock screw

Pallet cock

CLOCK TRAIN

Crutch screw

Pallet arbor

Pallet screw

Suspension spring

Crutch

Pallet

Escape wheel

Mainspring

Mainspring barrel cap

Pinion

FRONT PLATE

Third wheel

Pinion

Pendulum rod

Pinion

Center wheel

Mainspring barrel

Fusee

Fusee chain

Lenticular bob

Pivot hole

Fusee stop screw

Fusee stop

Tension spring screw

Tension spring

Rating nut

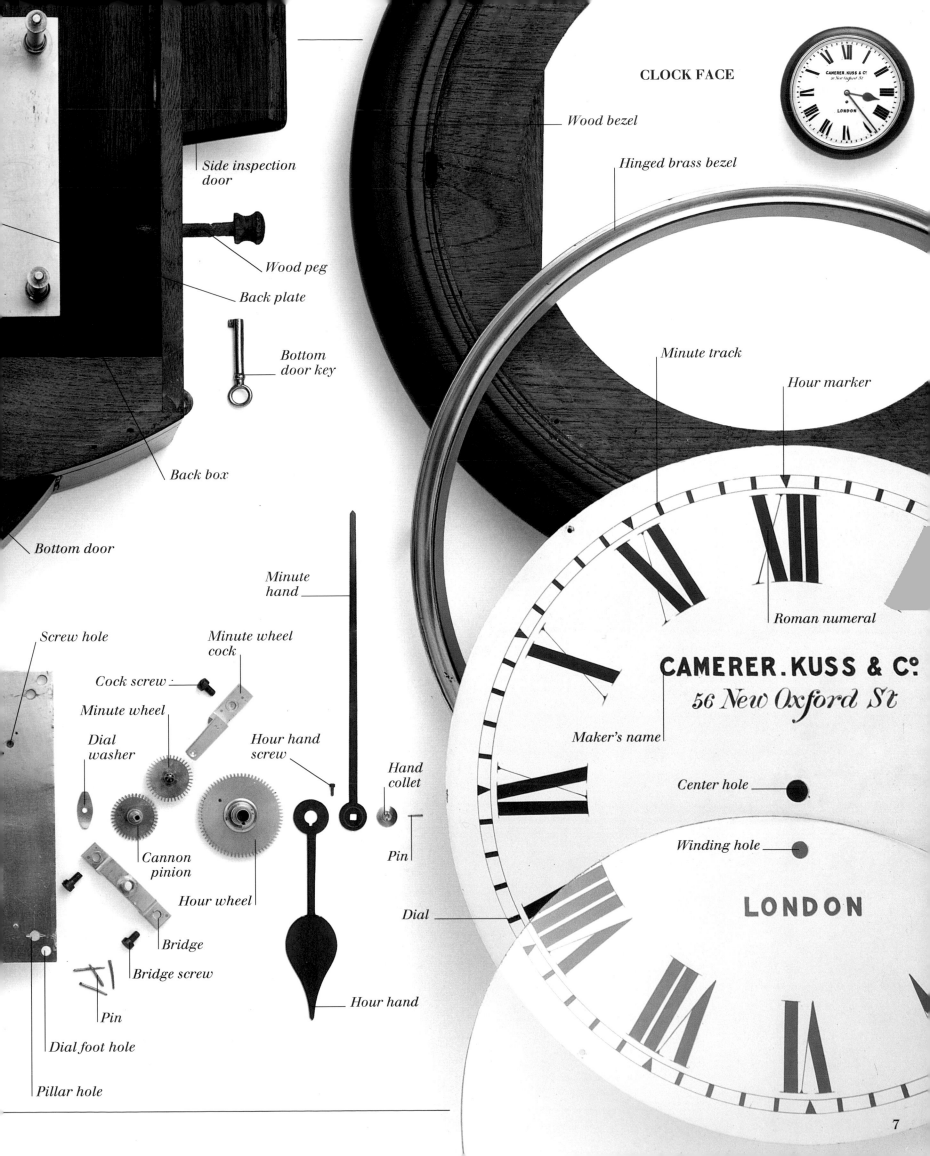

Side inspection door

Wood peg

Back plate

Bottom door key

Back box

Bottom door

Minute hand

Screw hole

Minute wheel cock

Cock screw

Minute wheel

Dial washer

Hour hand screw

Hand collet

Cannon pinion

Hour wheel

Pin

Bridge

Bridge screw

Pin

Dial foot hole

Pillar hole

Hour hand

Dial

CLOCK FACE

Wood bezel

Hinged brass bezel

Minute track

Hour marker

Roman numeral

CAMERER. KUSS & C?.
56 New Oxford St

Maker's name

Center hole

Winding hole

LONDON

7

Suit

A MAN'S TWO-PIECE SUIT IS A SET OF JACKET AND PANTS made in the same material; a three-piece suit has a vest as well. Many design details of modern suits hark back to previous centuries; for example, the vents at the back of a jacket made the garment hang better while the wearer was horseback riding. Suits are sold either ready-made or made-to-measure (known as bespoke). For a bespoke suit, the customer chooses the style and the cloth and the tailor measures the customer carefully. The tailor then makes up a pattern to these measurements and uses it as a guide for cutting the numerous pieces of fabric and lining needed for the suit.

JACKET

Top collar

Jacket hanger

Back

Stay tape

Forepart

Canvas

Lap hair

Back lining

Padding

Tailor tack

Brace button

Fastening

PANTS

Belt loop

Lining

Right leg back

Right leg front

RIGHT SLEEVE

Shoulder pad

Sleeve head wadding

Facing of lapel

INSIDE POCKET

Forepart lining

Lining

Under sleeve

Top sleeve

Lining

Cuff lining

Cuff button facing

Cuff button

Pocket flap and lining

Pocket lining

Coin pocket

SIDE POCKET

Pocket jet facing

Stay tape

Pocket facing

Pocket lining

8

COLLAR
- *Collar canvas*
- *Undercollar*
- *Back*
- *Stay tape*

BREAST POCKET
- *Pocket welt*
- *Lining*

TWO-PIECE SUIT
- *Notched lapel*
- *Hip flap pocket*

- *Facing of lapel*
- *Lap hair*
- *Padding*
- *Canvas*

- *Forepart lining*
- *Back lining*

- *Stay tape*

LEFT SLEEVE
- *Sleeve head wadding*
- *Shoulder pad*
- *Jacket button*
- *Lining*

WAISTBAND
- *Back curtain*
- *Trouser clasp*
- *Facing*
- *Left leg front*
- *Left leg back*
- *Fly button*

- *Forepart*

- *Pocket jet*
- *Pocket flap and lining*

- *Top sleeve*

- *Button*
- *French bearer*

- *Facing*
- *Canvas*
- *Material*

- *Cuff lining*
- *Lining*

- *Under sleeve*

HIP POCKET
- *Pocket jet facing*

SIDE POCKET
- *Pocket jet*
- *Pocket facing*
- *Stay tape*
- *Pocket facing*
- *Lining*

- *Cuff button facing*
- *Cuff button*

- *Button hole silk*
- *Gimp*

9

Telephone

A TELEPHONE MAKES IT POSSIBLE TO TALK to someone far away. It works by changing the voice's sound waves into electrical signals that travel very quickly along wires to another telephone. Each telephone has its own number, and to send a signal to someone you either dial their number or press the buttons on the key pad. When a signal arrives at a phone, it activates the tone ringer and this indicates that there is a call waiting to be answered. To talk to someone, you speak into the mouthpiece. The sound waves of your voice vibrate a thin metal disk inside the microphone, and this alters the electrical signal. When the signal reaches the other person's telephone, it travels along wires to an electromagnet in the receiver. The electromagnet moves a diaphragm which vibrates the surrounding air so that it sounds like the caller's voice.

Screw

Rubber sealing washer

Earpiece transducer

Dustcover for earpiece

Keypad membrane

Printed circuit board

PUSH BUTTON KEY PAD

Decorative plastic trim

Keytop

Screw

Carbon contact

Earpiece

Screw

Redial button

Memory button

Window

Key pad casing

Dustcover for mouthpiece

Handset front cover

Screw

Screw

Number list

TELEPHONE HANDSET

Top casing

Screw

Mouthpiece

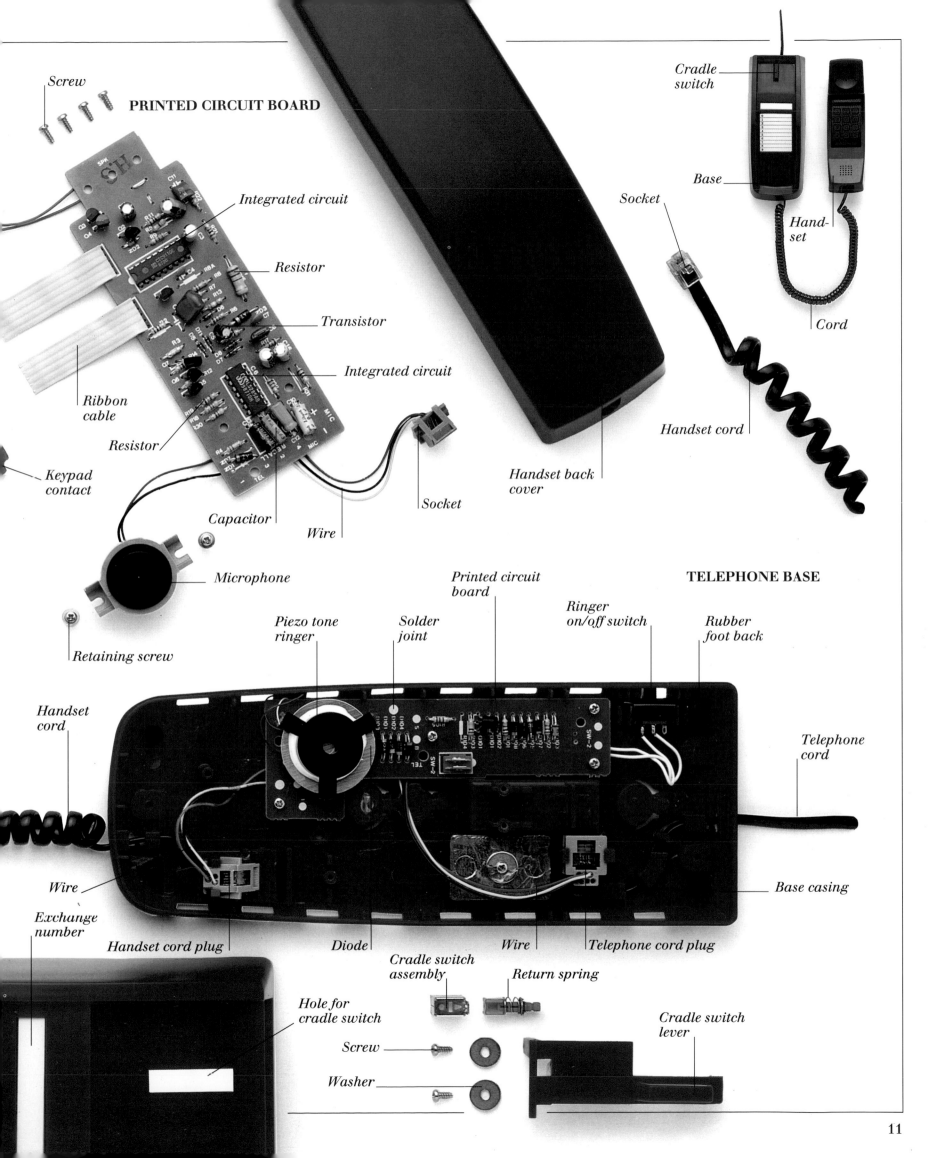

PRINTED CIRCUIT BOARD

Screw

Integrated circuit

Resistor

Transistor

Integrated circuit

Ribbon cable

Resistor

Keypad contact

Capacitor

Wire

Socket

Microphone

Retaining screw

Cradle switch

Base

Socket

Hand-set

Cord

Handset cord

Handset back cover

TELEPHONE BASE

Handset cord

Piezo tone ringer

Solder joint

Printed circuit board

Ringer on/off switch

Rubber foot back

Telephone cord

Wire

Exchange number

Handset cord plug

Diode

Wire

Telephone cord plug

Base casing

Hole for cradle switch

Cradle switch assembly

Return spring

Cradle switch lever

Screw

Washer

Pencils and pens

PENCILS AND PENS ARE USED for writing and drawing. Pencils have the advantage that any mistakes can be easily rubbed out. We commonly call them "lead pencils" but this term is a misnomer because the main ingredient of the "lead" is graphite, a form of carbon. The graphite is mixed with clay and fired in an oven; the more clay a pencil has, the paler the line drawn. In simple pencils the lead is encased in a wood stick that has to be sharpened. Mechanical pencils have metal or plastic cases; when you press the cap, or twist the tip of the cap, the lead appears. Fountain pens have a reservoir that holds ink and a nib through which ink flows on to the paper. When you use a fountain pen, the width of the nib, the pressure you exert, and the consistency of the ink all affect the thickness of the line drawn. Ballpoint pens are less versatile but generally more popular because they are easier to use. When you write or draw with a ballpoint pen, a ball in the nib rotates, allowing a small amount of thick ink to ooze out.

TYPES OF PENCILS AND PENS

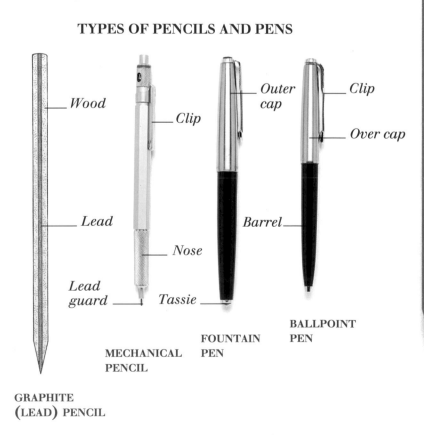

Wood

Lead

Lead guard

Clip

Nose

Tassie

MECHANICAL PENCIL

Outer cap

Barrel

FOUNTAIN PEN

Clip

Over cap

BALLPOINT PEN

GRAPHITE (LEAD) PENCIL

GRAPHITE (LEAD) PENCIL

MECHANICAL PENCIL

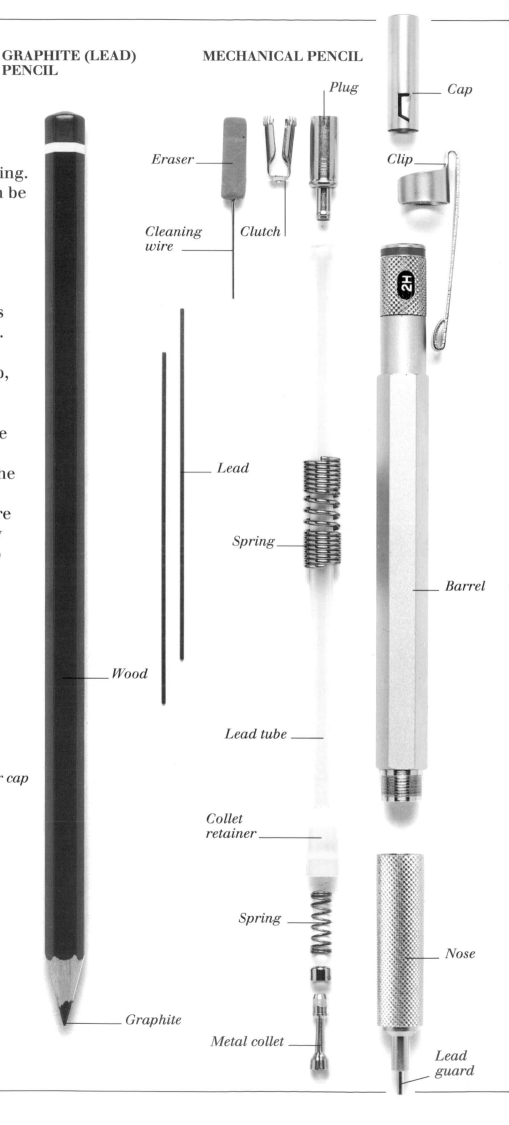

Plug

Cap

Eraser

Clip

Cleaning wire

Clutch

Lead

Spring

Barrel

Wood

Lead tube

Collet retainer

Spring

Nose

Graphite

Metal collet

Lead guard

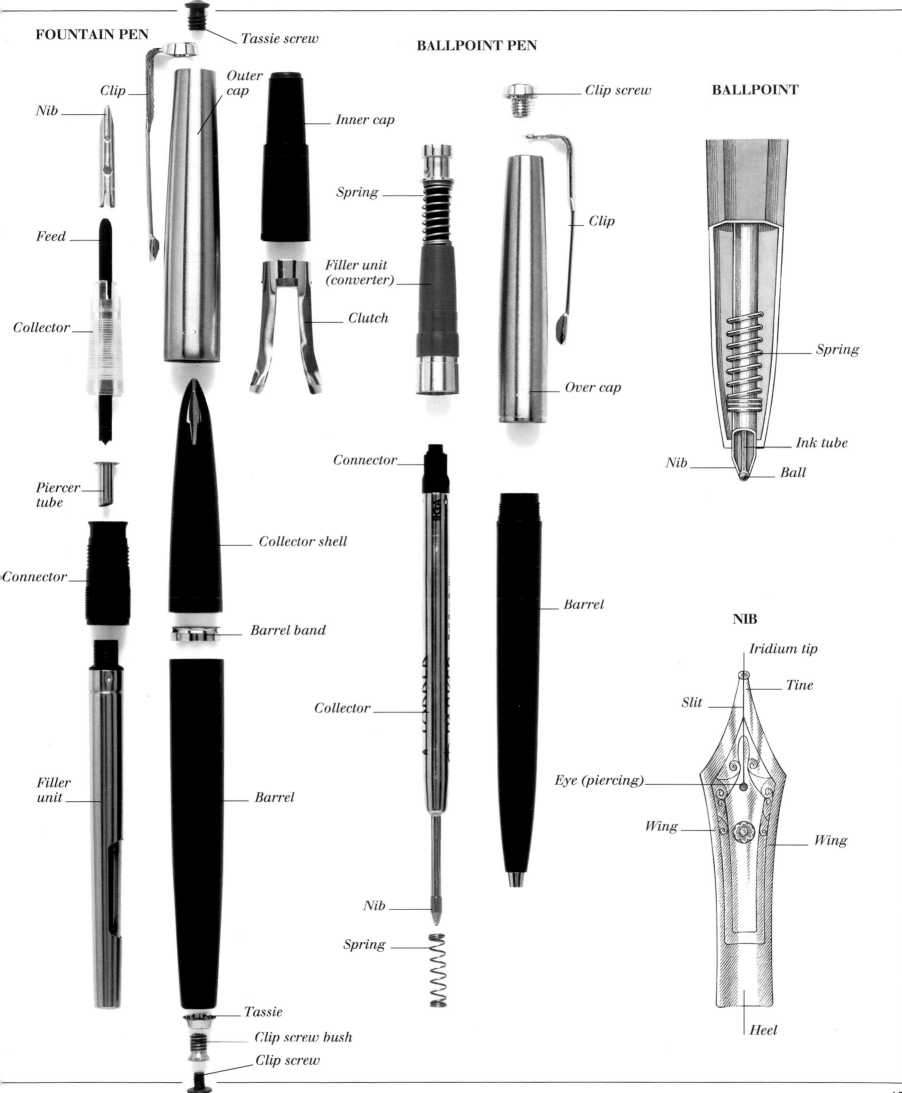

FOUNTAIN PEN

Tassie screw

Clip

Outer cap

Nib

Feed

Collector

Piercer tube

Connector

Filler unit

Barrel

Tassie

Clip screw bush

Clip screw

BALLPOINT PEN

Inner cap

Spring

Filler unit (converter)

Clutch

Clip screw

Clip

Over cap

Connector

Collector shell

Barrel band

Connector

Collector

Barrel

Nib

Spring

BALLPOINT

Spring

Nib

Ink tube

Ball

NIB

Iridium tip

Tine

Slit

Eye (piercing)

Wing

Wing

Heel

Personal stereo

A PERSONAL STEREO IS A SMALL, BATTERY-POWERED, portable cassette player that reproduces sound recorded on magnetic tape. A cassette, holding tape wound on two reels, slots into the machine so that the reels fit over two spindles. Pressing the "play" button causes a pinch roller and a capstan to rotate and drive the tape over the playback head, while the reels supply the tape and take up the slack. A magnetic pattern, representing sound, is recorded onto the tape. When the playback head comes into contact with the tape, a weak electric current is induced in it by the pattern. The current, which becomes weaker or stronger as the pattern varies, is sent through an amplifier and then to the earphones. In each earphone, the current is converted into a magnetic field that vibrates a small cone, and these vibrations produce sound waves. Stereo sound is reproduced by recording two magnetic patterns, or tracks, one for the left and one for the right ear.

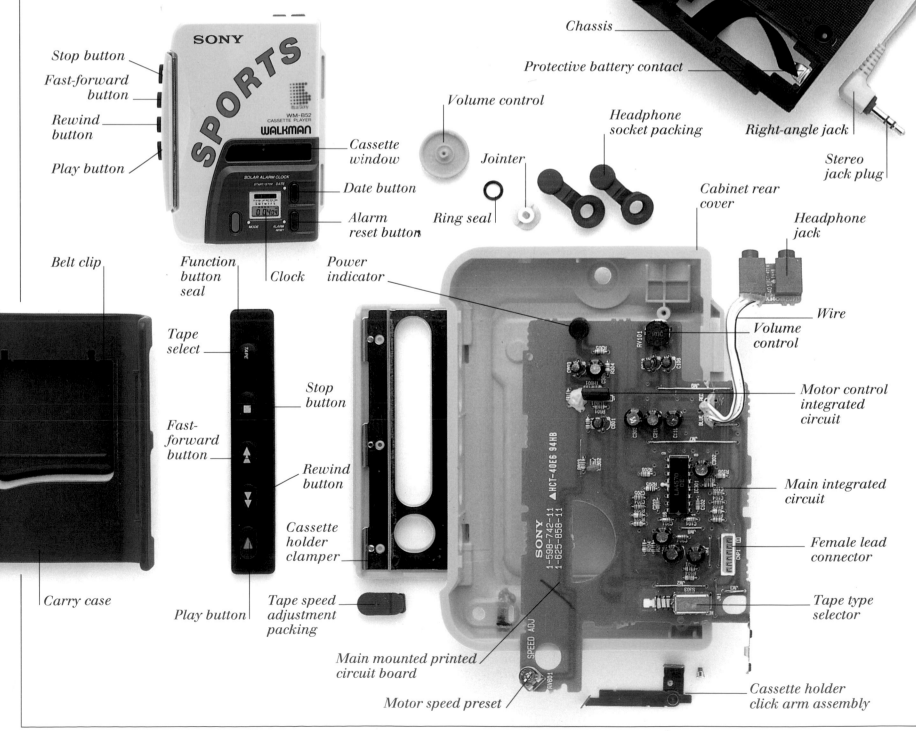

Spring

Chassis

Protective battery contact

Stop button

Fast-forward button

Rewind button

Play button

SONY
SPORTS
WM-B52
CASSETTE PLAYER
WALKMAN

SOLAR ALARM CLOCK
START/STOP DATE

Cassette window

Volume control

Headphone socket packing

Right-angle jack

Stereo jack plug

Date button

Jointer

Alarm reset button

Ring seal

Cabinet rear cover

Headphone jack

Belt clip

Function button seal

Clock

Power indicator

Wire

Volume control

Tape select

Stop button

Motor control integrated circuit

Fast-forward button

Rewind button

Main integrated circuit

Cassette holder clamper

Female lead connector

Carry case

Play button

Tape speed adjustment packing

Tape type selector

Main mounted printed circuit board

Motor speed preset

Cassette holder click arm assembly

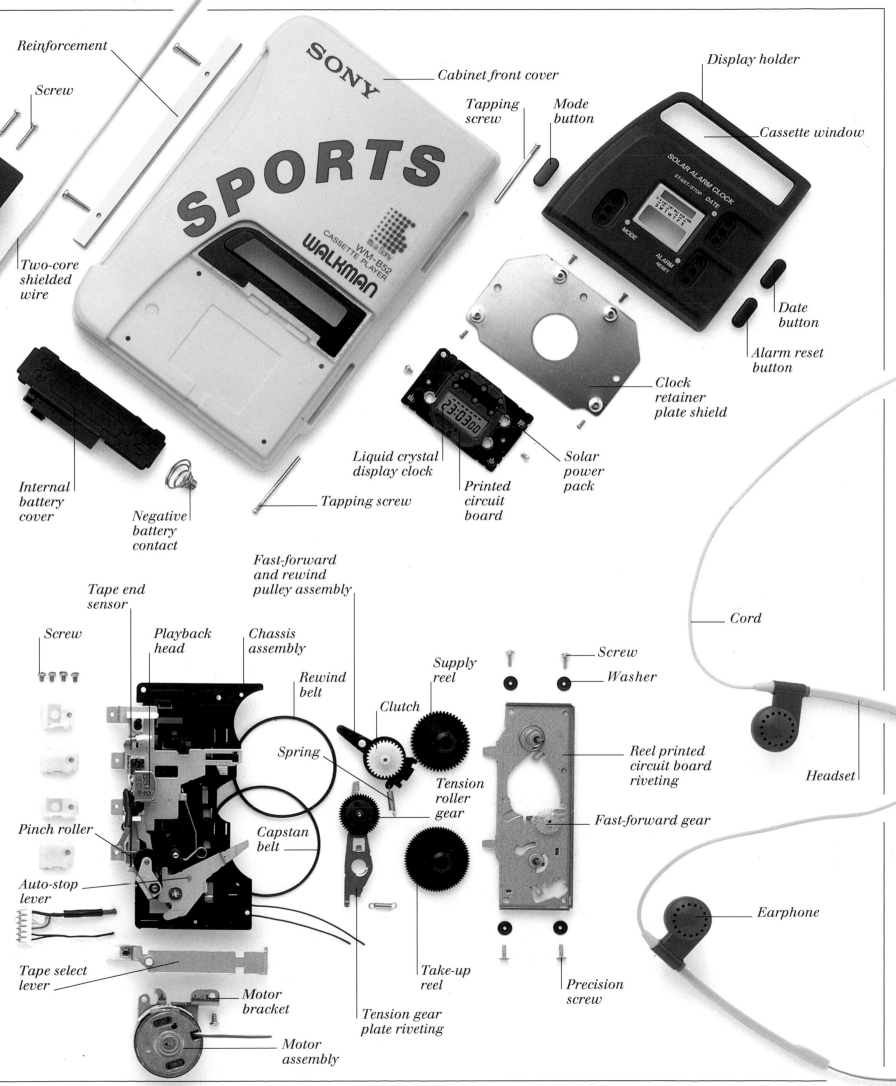

Reinforcement

Screw

Two-core shielded wire

Internal battery cover

Negative battery contact

SONY

SPORTS

WALKMAN
CASSETTE PLAYER
WM-B52

Cabinet front cover

Tapping screw

Mode button

Liquid crystal display clock

Tapping screw

Printed circuit board

Solar power pack

Display holder

SOLAR ALARM CLOCK

Cassette window

Date button

Alarm reset button

Clock retainer plate shield

Screw

Tape end sensor

Playback head

Chassis assembly

Fast-forward and rewind pulley assembly

Rewind belt

Clutch

Spring

Capstan belt

Pinch roller

Auto-stop lever

Tape select lever

Motor bracket

Motor assembly

Tension gear plate riveting

Supply reel

Tension roller gear

Take-up reel

Screw

Washer

Reel printed circuit board riveting

Fast-forward gear

Precision screw

Cord

Headset

Earphone

Batteries

CONVENIENT, PORTABLE SOURCES of electricity are usually known as batteries, although most of them should really be called "power cells." Strictly speaking, a battery is a set of power cells used together. Of the examples shown here, only the car battery is a true battery as it contains several cells in one case. All the others are single power cells. Most batteries, including the commonly used alkaline manganese cells and most button batteries, must be replaced when the chemicals they contain no longer provide electricity. Other batteries, such as nickel-cadmium cells and lead acid car batteries, are rechargeable and can be used over and over again.

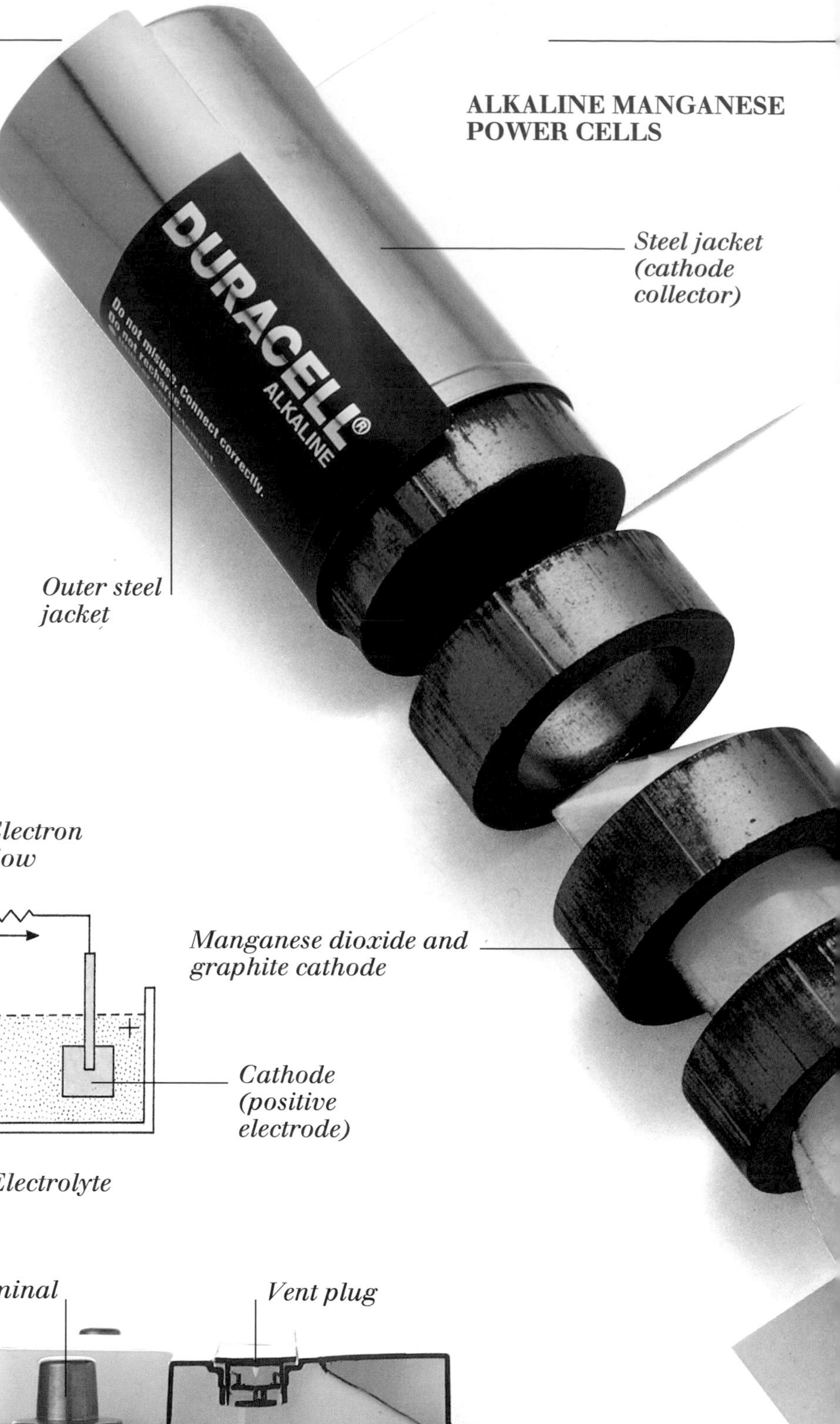

ALKALINE MANGANESE POWER CELLS

Steel jacket (cathode collector)

Outer steel jacket

Manganese dioxide and graphite cathode

HOW A POWER CELL WORKS

All power cells consist of two electrodes immersed in a chemical powder or liquid called an electrolyte. They produce a current by converting chemical energy into electrical energy. Electrons flow from the anode (negative electrode) to the cathode (positive electrode). In some cells, the electrolyte is absorbed into the material of the anode and cathode.

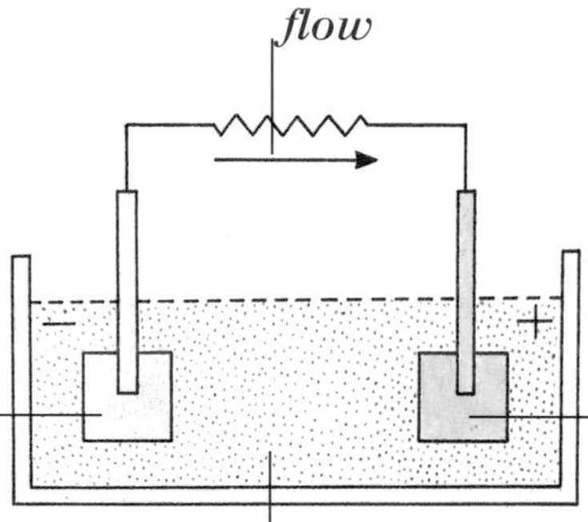

Electron flow

Anode (negative electrode)

Cathode (positive electrode)

Electrolyte

LEAD ACID CAR BATTERY

Negative terminal

Positive terminal

Positive terminal

Vent plug

Lead metal negative plate

Cell divider

Plate separator

Battery cover

Lead oxide positive plate

16

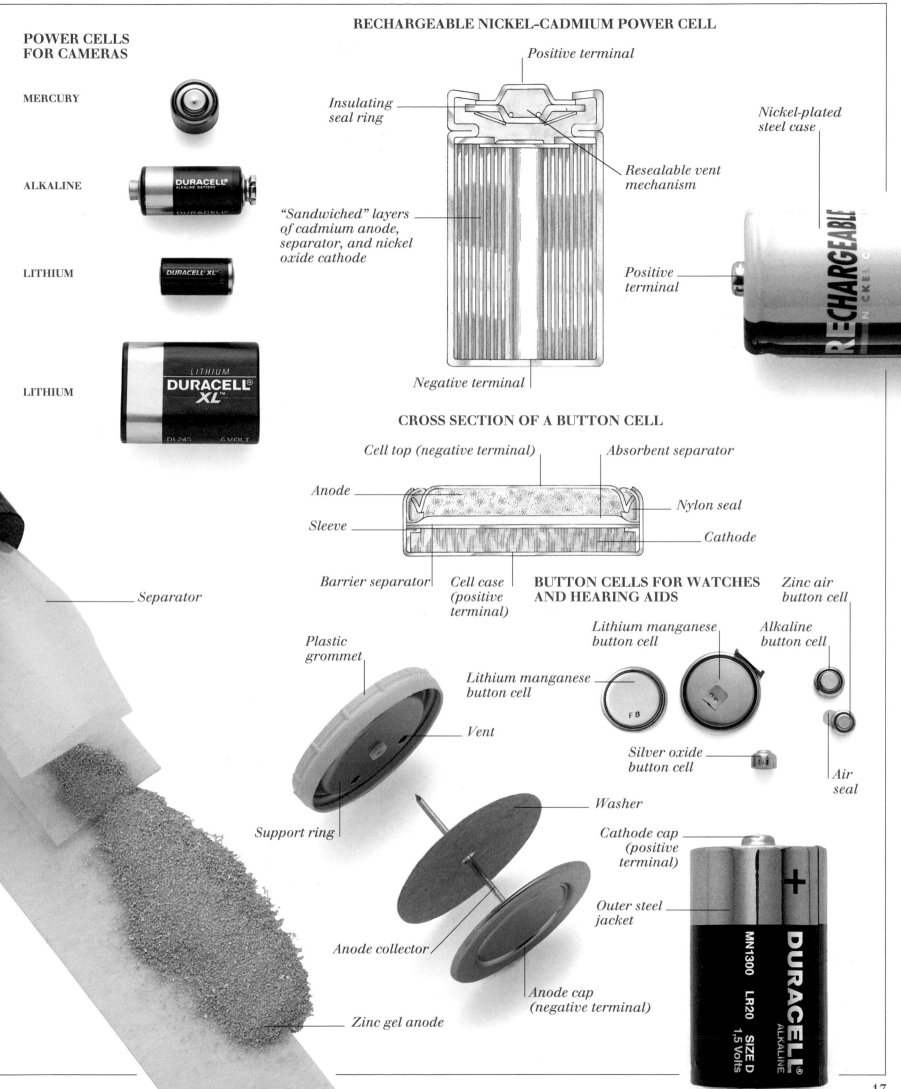

POWER CELLS FOR CAMERAS

MERCURY

ALKALINE

LITHIUM

LITHIUM

RECHARGEABLE NICKEL-CADMIUM POWER CELL

Positive terminal

Insulating seal ring

Resealable vent mechanism

Nickel-plated steel case

"Sandwiched" layers of cadmium anode, separator, and nickel oxide cathode

Positive terminal

Negative terminal

CROSS SECTION OF A BUTTON CELL

Cell top (negative terminal)

Absorbent separator

Anode

Nylon seal

Sleeve

Cathode

Barrier separator

Cell case (positive terminal)

BUTTON CELLS FOR WATCHES AND HEARING AIDS

Zinc air button cell

Lithium manganese button cell

Alkaline button cell

Lithium manganese button cell

Silver oxide button cell

Air seal

Separator

Plastic grommet

Vent

Support ring

Washer

Cathode cap (positive terminal)

Outer steel jacket

Anode collector

Anode cap (negative terminal)

Zinc gel anode

MN1300

LR20

SIZE D

1.5 Volts

DURACELL

ALKALINE

17

Fishing tackle

MANY ANGLERS USE A BEWILDERING variety of tackle, but the fundamental items needed for fishing are a rod, reel, line, and lure. The angler uses the rod, reel, and line to cast the lure over the water. The reel controls the line as it spills off the spool and as it is wound back. Some reels have a gearing system that provides the power for reeling in fighting fish. Weights, sometimes called sinkers or leads, may be attached to the line so that it will sink to the required depth. Swivels are attached to prevent the line from twisting. The lure, whether artificial or real bait, must fool the fish into trying to attack or eat it. Artificial flies often imitate the appearance, movement, and sometimes the scent of the prey on which some fish feed. When a fish bites, the hook must become embedded in its mouth and remain there while the catch is reeled in.

Keeper ring

Drag spindle

Handgrip

Disk drag

Drag washer

Disk spring

Gear retainer

Dual click gear

Retaining screw

Check slide

Check pawl cover

Check pawl

Check spring

REELS

Spool-release button

Reel foot (reel scoop)

Plate-nut

Click mechanism

Mechanical brake

Side plate

Centrifugal brake

Spool

Handle

Star drag

Level-wind system

MULTIPLIER REEL

HOOKS, SWIVELS, AND WEIGHTS

Eye

Shank

Gape   ANATOMY OF A HOOK

Bend

Throat

Point

Barb

Line

Reel foot (reel scoop)

Unskirted spool

Handle

TREBLE HOOK

ABERDEEN HOOK

REVERSED BEND HOOK

Tension nut (drag adjustment)

Ratchet (anti-reverse device)

Handgrip

EXAMPLES OF BARREL SWIVELS

HILLMAN ANTI-KINK WEIGHT

Reel

Bail arm

FIXED-SPOOL REEL

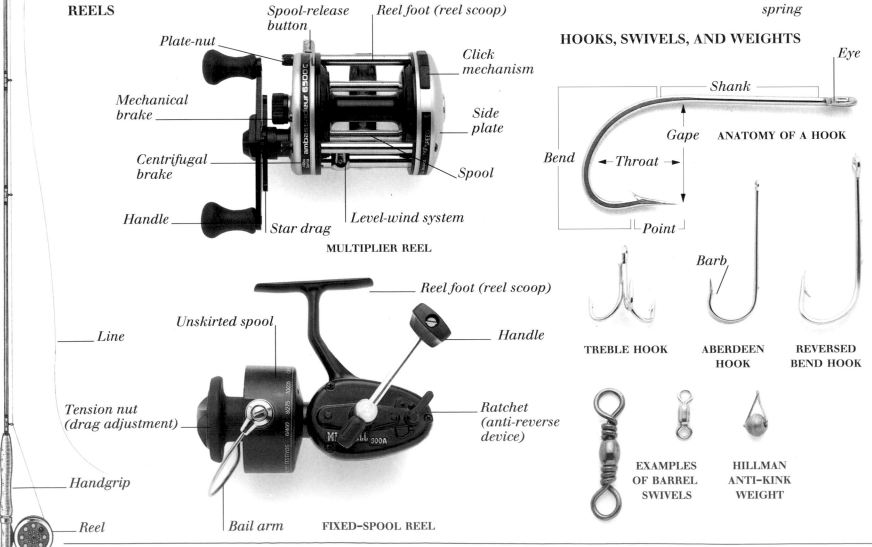

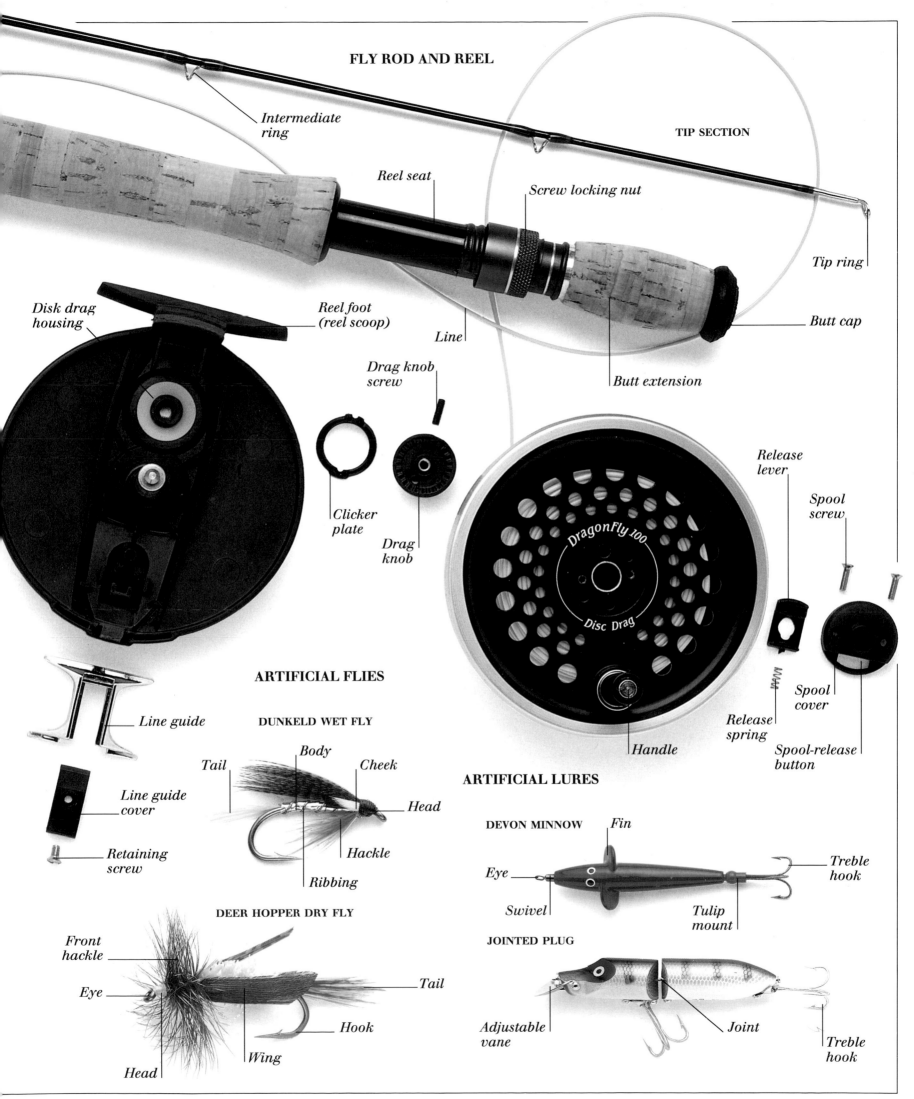

FLY ROD AND REEL

Intermediate ring

TIP SECTION

Reel seat

Screw locking nut

Tip ring

Disk drag housing

Reel foot (reel scoop)

Line

Butt cap

Drag knob screw

Butt extension

Release lever

Spool screw

Clicker plate

Drag knob

DragonFly 100

Disc Drag

Line guide

ARTIFICIAL FLIES

DUNKELD WET FLY

Tail

Body

Cheek

Head

Release spring

Spool cover

Line guide cover

Hackle

Spool-release button

Retaining screw

Ribbing

ARTIFICIAL LURES

DEVON MINNOW

Fin

Handle

DEER HOPPER DRY FLY

Eye

Treble hook

Front hackle

Eye

Tail

Swivel

Tulip mount

JOINTED PLUG

Hook

Joint

Adjustable vane

Head

Wing

Treble hook

Drills

THE ELECTRICALLY POWERED MOTOR OF A POWER DRILL, cooled by a fan, turns a shaft at high speed. The shaft connects, in turn, to a system of gears that rotates a chuck even faster. Clamped by the chuck, a sharp drill bit cuts out the hole, and at the same time the bit's screw-shaped grooves channel the waste out of the hole. For drilling hard materials, many power drills have a hammer mechanism; when this is operated a ratchet in the gearcase causes the chuck and bit to pound in and out as they drill. A hand drill, although slower and less forceful than a power drill, is easier to control. For cutting wide holes, carpenters often prefer a brace-and-bit. This acts like a lever: the bowed handle of the brace moves a larger distance than the bit, turning the bit with extra force.

MOTOR ASSEMBLY

Commutator

Armature

Armature spindle

Fan

Motor case

Motor case

Field

Brush spring

Screw

Washer

Brush

Lead wire to motor

Brush holder

Top insert blank

Hammer mechanism actuator

Electromagnetic induction capacitor

Screw hole

Hammer actuator position

Gearcase position

Chuck key holder

Switch

Motor position

Screw

INTERNAL VIEW OF HOUSING COVER

Lock button

Switch trigger

Trigger position

TRIGGER MECHANISM

Washer

Cable cordset

Spring

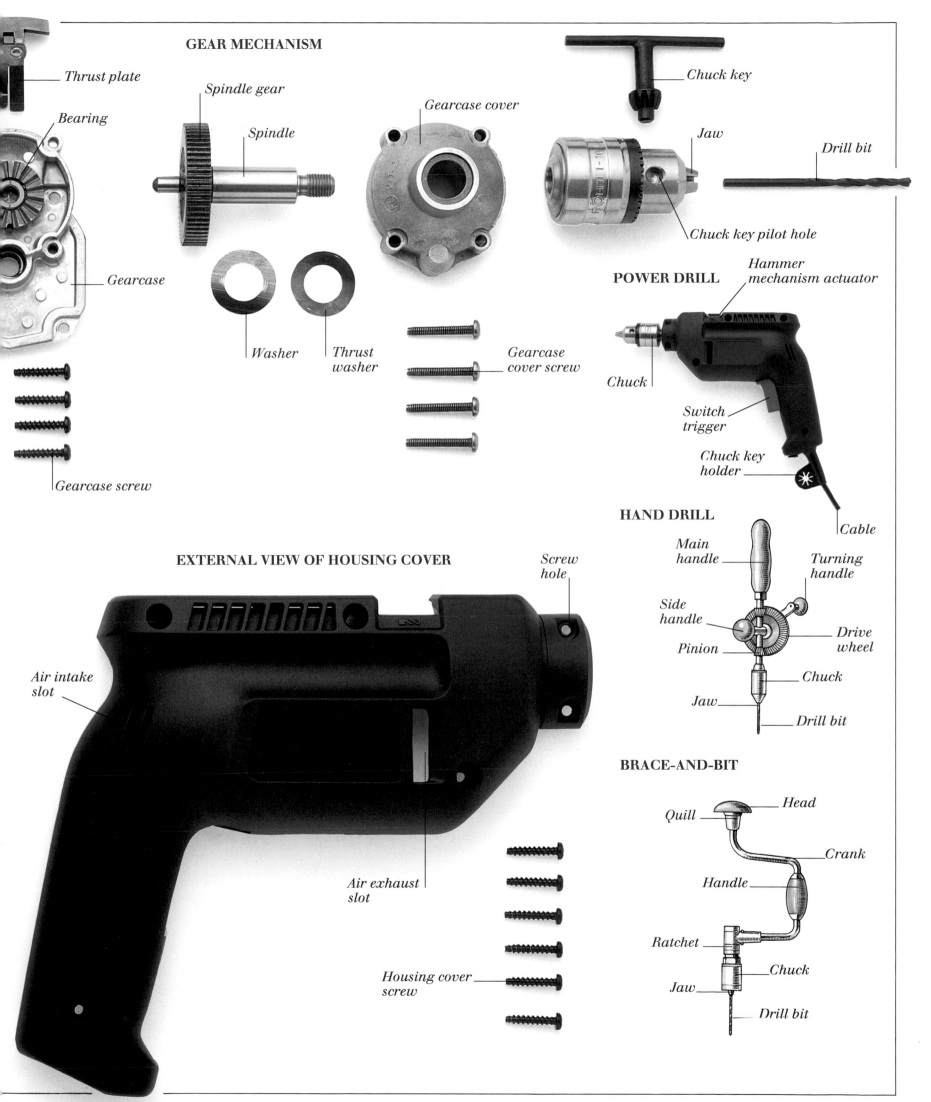

GEAR MECHANISM

Thrust plate

Bearing

Gearcase

Gearcase screw

Spindle gear

Spindle

Washer

Thrust washer

Gearcase cover

Gearcase cover screw

Chuck key

Jaw

Chuck key pilot hole

Drill bit

POWER DRILL

Hammer mechanism actuator

Chuck

Switch trigger

Chuck key holder

Cable

HAND DRILL

Main handle

Turning handle

Side handle

Pinion

Drive wheel

Chuck

Jaw

Drill bit

EXTERNAL VIEW OF HOUSING COVER

Screw hole

Air intake slot

Air exhaust slot

Housing cover screw

BRACE-AND-BIT

Quill

Head

Crank

Handle

Ratchet

Chuck

Jaw

Drill bit

Shoes

WELL MADE SHOES PROTECT THE FEET and are also comfortable and long lasting. The best shoemakers use a wood or plastic mold, called a last, which matches the shape of the customer's foot. The different parts of a shoe are stitched and glued together around the last; rivets and nails are used only in the heel, which is built up from layers of leather and rubber. The steel shank gives support to the arch of the foot and, with the seat lift, helps the wearer maintain posture. The layers of the sole give strength, while the soft insole cushions the foot. The leather welt sewn between the leather uppers and the sole ensures a strong join.

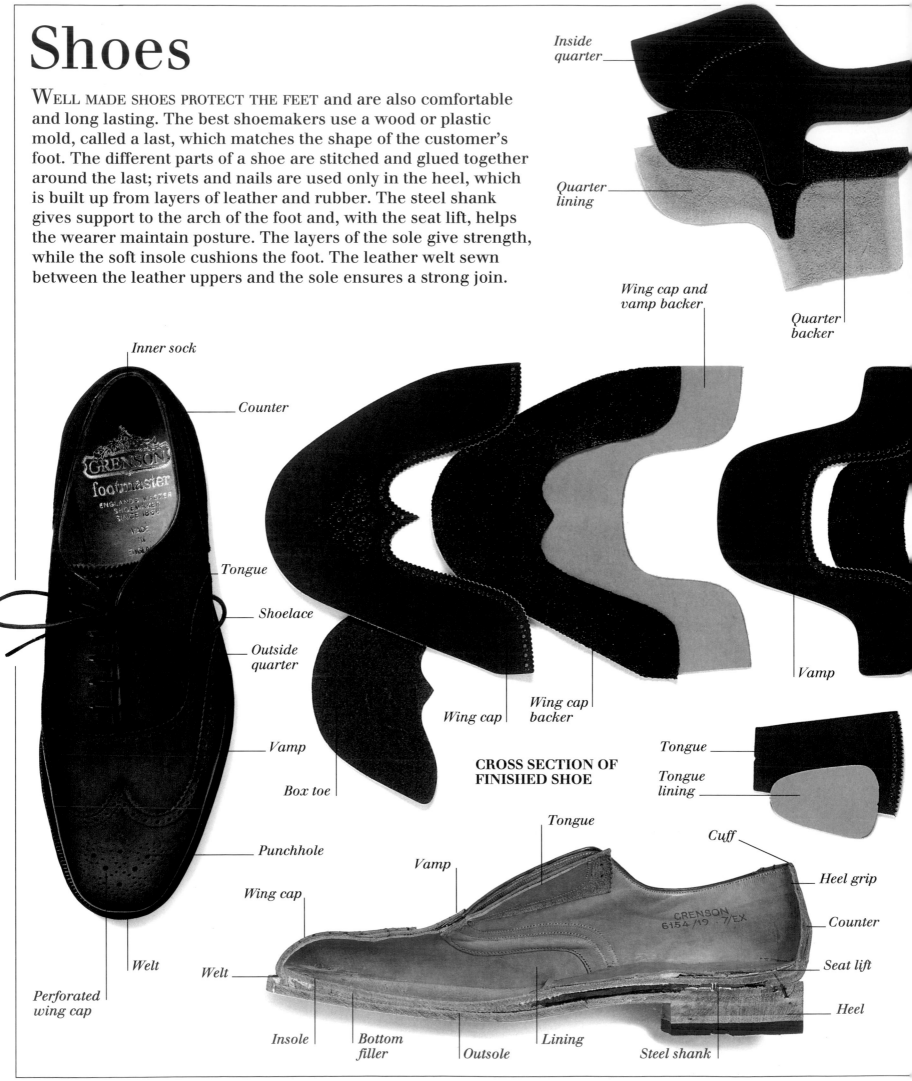

Inside quarter

Quarter lining

Quarter backer

Wing cap and vamp backer

Inner sock

Counter

Tongue

Shoelace

Outside quarter

Vamp

Box toe

Wing cap

Wing cap backer

Vamp

CROSS SECTION OF FINISHED SHOE

Tongue

Tongue lining

Punchhole

Welt

Perforated wing cap

Wing cap

Welt

Insole

Bottom filler

Outsole

Vamp

Tongue

Lining

Cuff

Heel grip

Counter

Seat lift

Heel

Steel shank

GRENSON 6154/19 7/EX

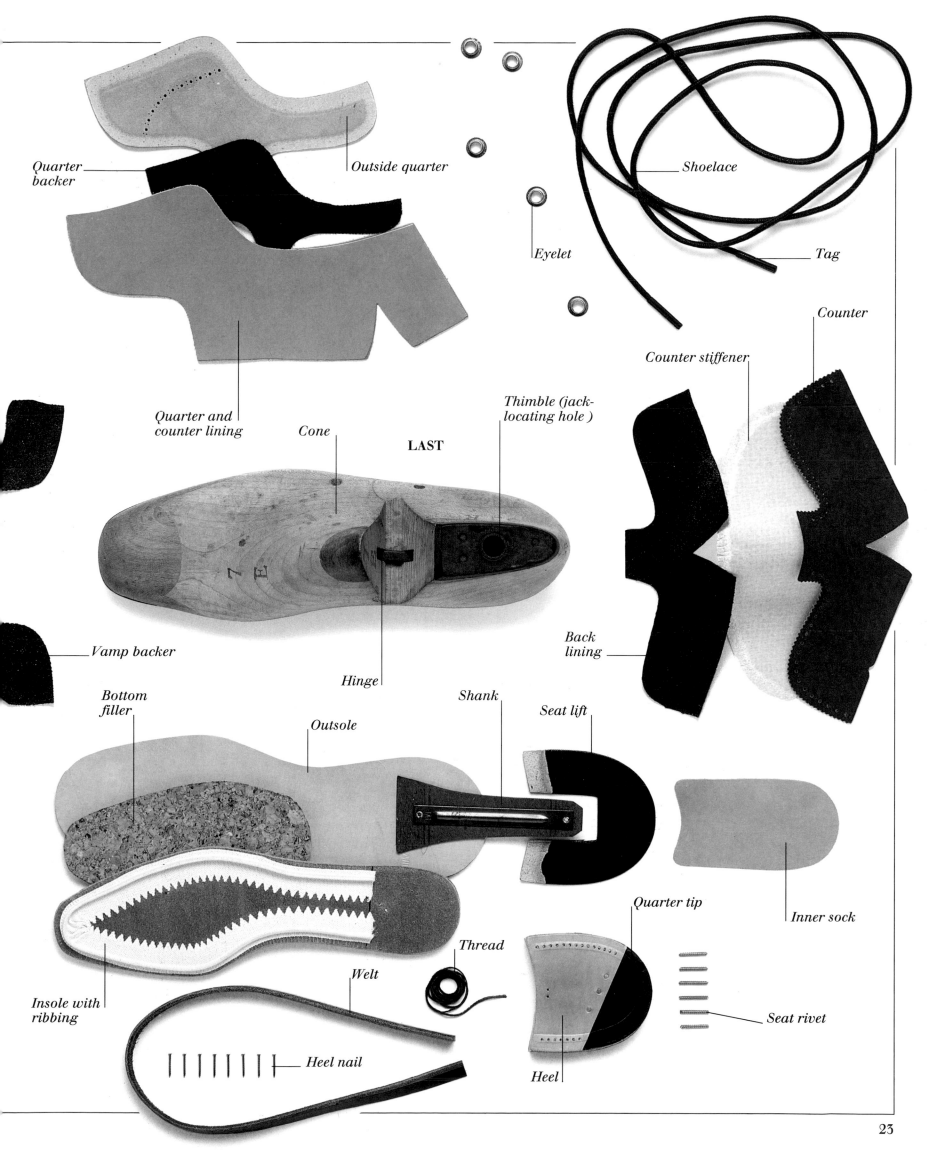

Quarter backer

Outside quarter

Shoelace

Eyelet

Tag

Counter

Counter stiffener

Quarter and counter lining

Cone

LAST

Thimble (jack-locating hole)

Vamp backer

Hinge

Back lining

Bottom filler

Outsole

Shank

Seat lift

Quarter tip

Inner sock

Thread

Insole with ribbing

Welt

Seat rivet

Heel nail

Heel

Shavers and razors

ALL SHAVERS AND RAZORS GIVE A SMOOTH shave by cutting hair as close to the skin as possible without causing injury. The most basic razor is a barber's cut-throat, an extremely sharp open blade. The cut-throat has the advantage that it can be resharpened when blunt; a drawback is that it can inflict a serious wound. Because of this danger the safety razor was invented. Its disposable blade is protected by a guard that prevents deep cuts to the skin. Safer still is the electric shaver. The rechargeable one shown here has two blade screen combs in the shaving head, which hold the hairs as the rotating blades, or cutters, cut them, while a sprung drive shaft ensures that the blades cut close to the screen combs. A beardtrimmer, on the side of the shaver, has two serrated blades, one of which slides sideways over the other.

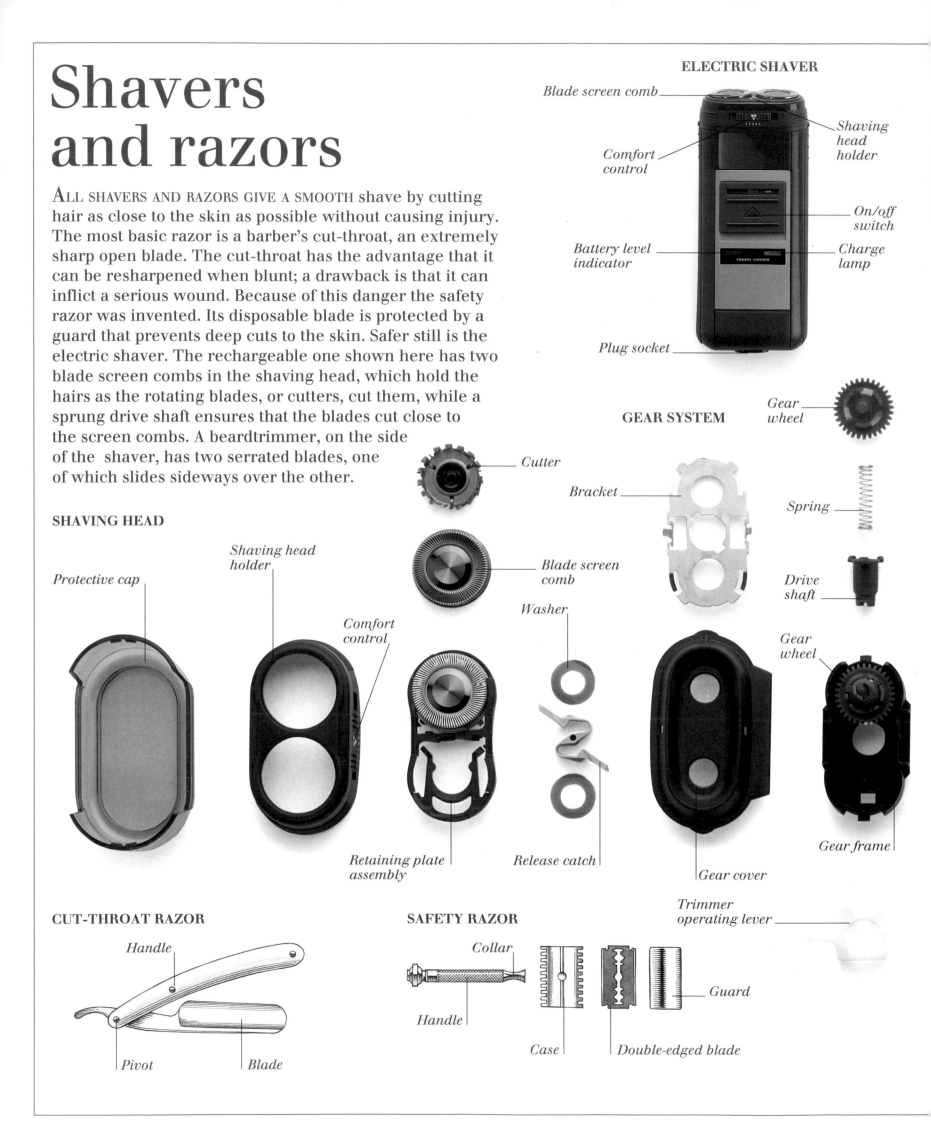

ELECTRIC SHAVER

Blade screen comb
Shaving head holder
Comfort control
On/off switch
Battery level indicator
Charge lamp
Plug socket

GEAR SYSTEM

Gear wheel
Cutter
Bracket
Spring
Blade screen comb
Drive shaft
Washer
Gear wheel
Gear frame
Gear cover
Retaining plate assembly
Release catch
Trimmer operating lever

SHAVING HEAD

Protective cap
Shaving head holder
Comfort control

CUT-THROAT RAZOR

Handle
Pivot
Blade

SAFETY RAZOR

Collar
Handle
Guard
Case
Double-edged blade

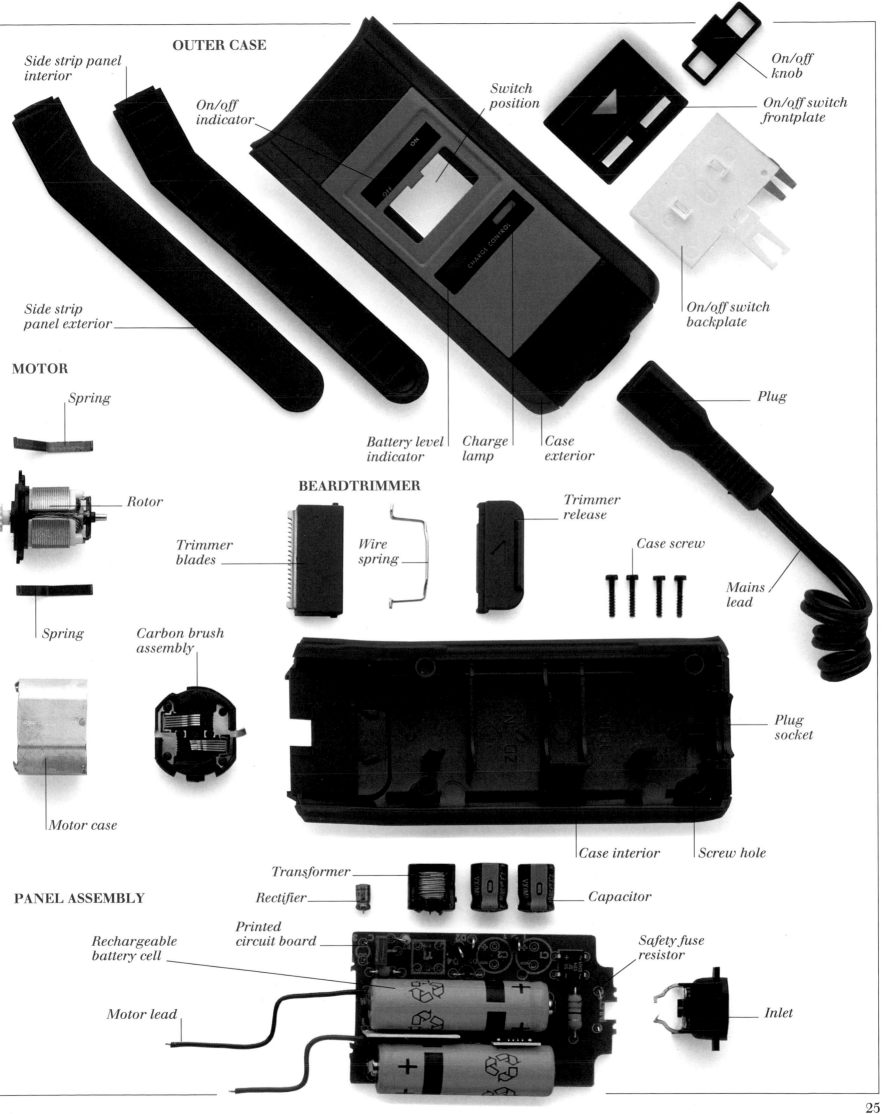

OUTER CASE

Side strip panel interior

On/off indicator

Switch position

On/off knob

On/off switch frontplate

Side strip panel exterior

On/off switch backplate

MOTOR

Spring

Rotor

Plug

Battery level indicator

Charge lamp

Case exterior

BEARDTRIMMER

Trimmer blades

Wire spring

Trimmer release

Case screw

Spring

Carbon brush assembly

Mains lead

Motor case

Plug socket

Case interior

Screw hole

PANEL ASSEMBLY

Transformer

Rectifier

Capacitor

Printed circuit board

Rechargeable battery cell

Safety fuse resistor

Motor lead

Inlet

Books

THOUGH THE PROCESS OF BOOKBINDING today is usually mechanized, some books are still bound by hand. The pages of a book are printed on large sheets of paper called sections, or signatures. When folded, sections usually make 8, 16, or 32 pages. To assemble a hand-bound hardback book, the binder first places the folded sections in the correct order within the endpapers. Next, he or she sews the sections together along the spine edge using strong thread and then pastes them with glue for extra strength. After trimming the pages, the binder puts the book in a press and hammers the spine to shape it. The binder then glues one or more linings on the spine. The cover, or case, comes last. To make this, the bookbinder sticks cover boards to the endpapers, front and back, and then covers them with cloth or leather.

HALF-BOUND BOOK

Corner piece

Spine

Tail

Marbleized paper

LEATHER-BOUND BOOK

Joint

Leather cover

Fore edge

Rib

Spine

Tail

Ribbon

Gold tooling

HALF-BOUND BOOK

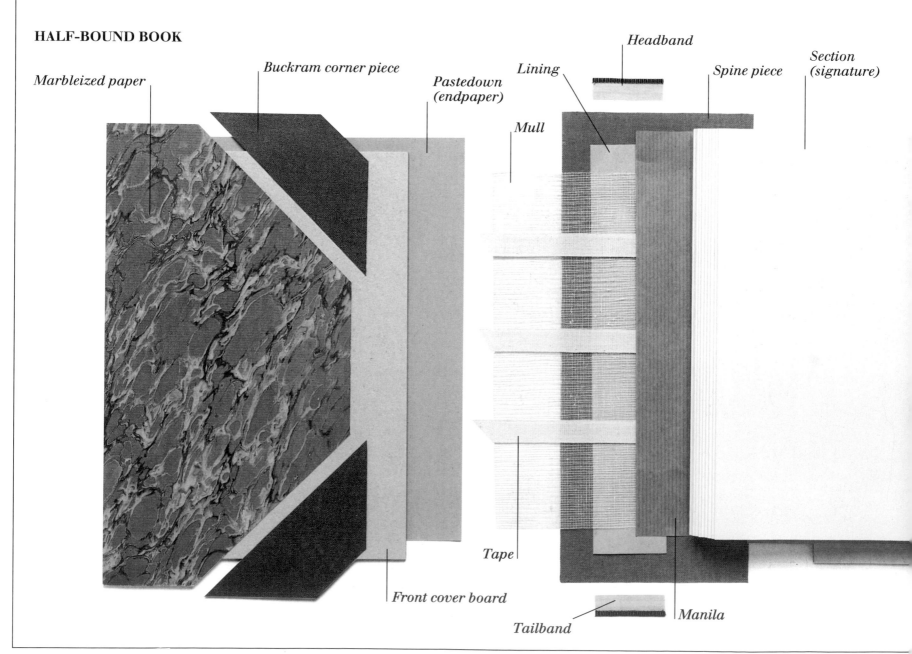

Marbleized paper

Buckram corner piece

Pastedown (endpaper)

Lining

Headband

Spine piece

Section (signature)

Mull

Tape

Front cover board

Tailband

Manila

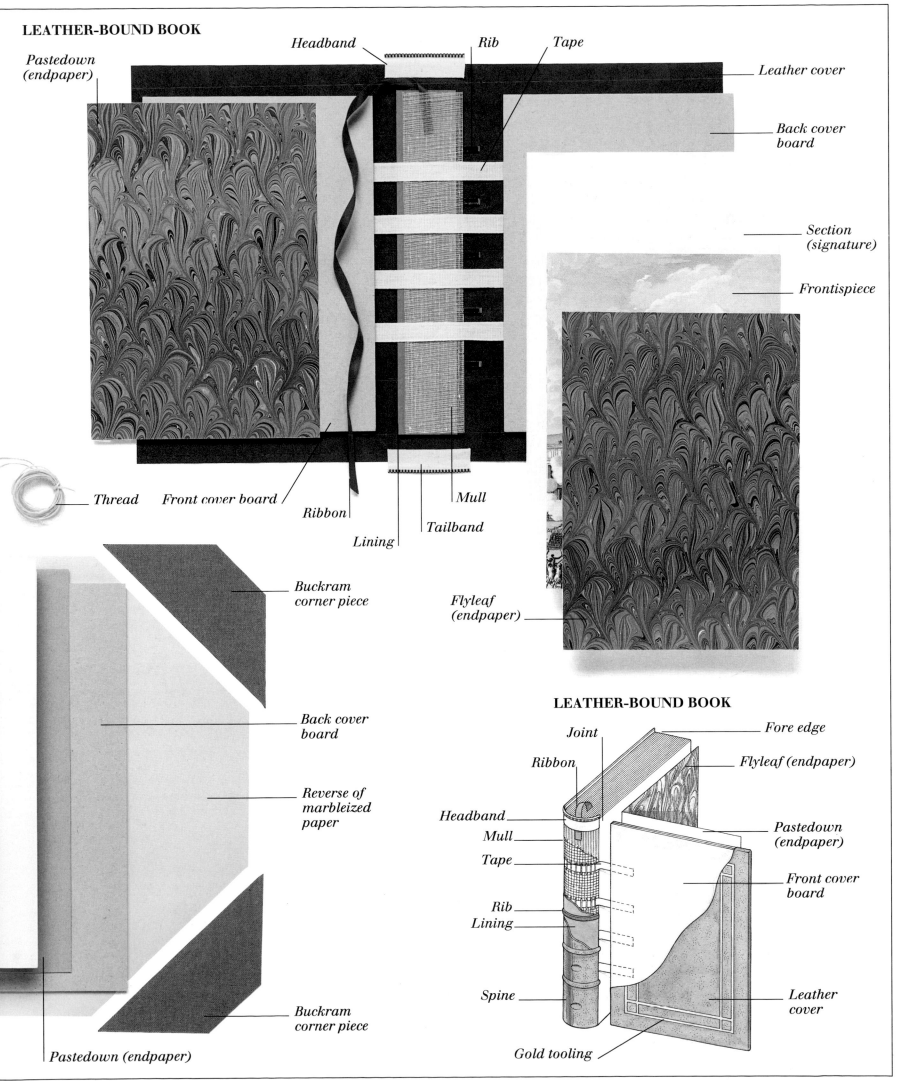

LEATHER-BOUND BOOK

Pastedown (endpaper)

Headband

Rib

Tape

Leather cover

Back cover board

Section (signature)

Frontispiece

Thread

Front cover board

Ribbon

Lining

Tailband

Mull

Flyleaf (endpaper)

Buckram corner piece

Back cover board

Reverse of marbleized paper

Buckram corner piece

Pastedown (endpaper)

LEATHER-BOUND BOOK

Joint

Ribbon

Fore edge

Flyleaf (endpaper)

Headband

Mull

Tape

Pastedown (endpaper)

Front cover board

Rib

Lining

Spine

Leather cover

Gold tooling

Camera

A CAMERA IS AN INSTRUMENT used for recording images on photographic film. It consists of a light-tight box with a shutter, a lens containing a diaphragm, and a viewing system. When the shutter is released, the film is exposed to light from the subject that is being photographed. Adjusting the shutter speed alters the time for which the film is exposed to light. The diaphragm, by altering the aperture of the lens, controls the intensity of light entering the camera. The total amount of light entering the camera is called the exposure. The lens focuses the light onto the film. When there is insufficient light to produce an adequate image, a flashgun may be used to give extra light.

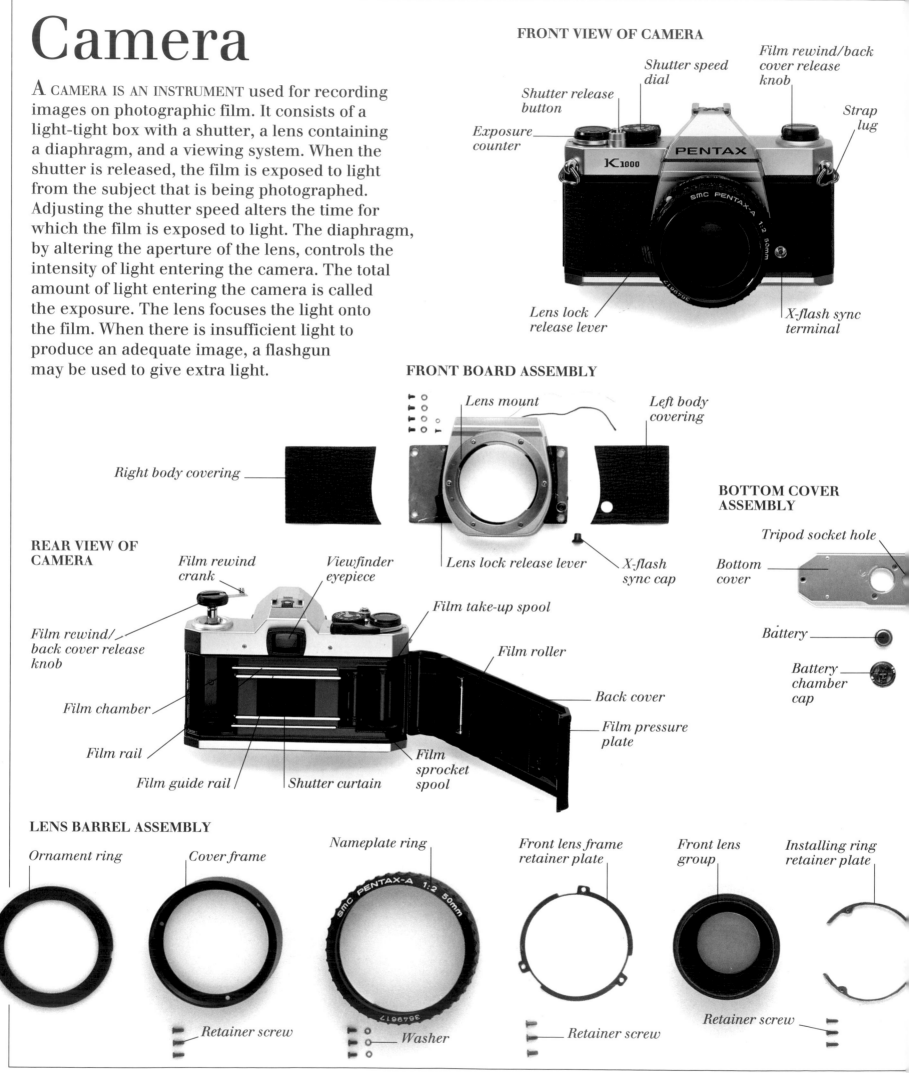

FRONT VIEW OF CAMERA

Shutter release button
Shutter speed dial
Film rewind/back cover release knob
Exposure counter
Strap lug
Lens lock release lever
X-flash sync terminal

FRONT BOARD ASSEMBLY

Lens mount
Left body covering
Right body covering
Lens lock release lever
X-flash sync cap

REAR VIEW OF CAMERA

Film rewind crank
Viewfinder eyepiece
Film take-up spool
Film rewind/back cover release knob
Film roller
Film chamber
Back cover
Film rail
Film pressure plate
Film guide rail
Shutter curtain
Film sprocket spool

BOTTOM COVER ASSEMBLY

Tripod socket hole
Bottom cover
Battery
Battery chamber cap

LENS BARREL ASSEMBLY

Ornament ring
Cover frame
Nameplate ring
Front lens frame retainer plate
Front lens group
Installing ring retainer plate
Retainer screw
Washer
Retainer screw
Retainer screw

TOP COVER ASSEMBLY

Counter dial cover

Exposure counter dial

Counter dial housing

Wind lever install spring

Film wind lever

Wind lever collar

Speed dial knob

Shutter dial knob spring

Film speed indicator

Shutter speed dial

Retainer screw

Top cover

X-contact

Hot shoe

Rewind shaft

Film rewind/ back cover release knob

Retainer screw

Washer

Window

Prism retainer plate

Shutter release button

Shutter speed index

Rewind shaft bushing

Film rewind crank

MAIN BODY

Prism retainer spring

Pentaprism

Cover frame

Retainer screw

Strap lug

Viewfinder eyepiece

Hole for film rewind button

Retainer screw

Film rewind crank

Film rewind/back cover release knob

TOP VIEW OF CAMERA

Focusing ring

Depth-of-field guide

Aperture auto-lock button

Aperture/distance index

Subject distance scale

Lens alignment node

Lens lock release lever

Shutter release button

Shutter cocked indicator

Exposure counter

Film wind lever

Shutter speed dial

Film speed indicator

Shutter speed index

X-contact

Hot shoe

ft m ∞ 10 15 3 8 2.6 1.5
22 16 8 4 4 8 16 22
A 22 16 11 8 5.6 4 2.82

Supporter ring retainer plate

Supporter ring

Diaphragm blade

Installing ring

Main barrel assembly

Rear lens group

Opening and closing plate

Teddy bear

NAMED FOR THE AMERICAN PRESIDENT and dedicated bear hunter, Theodore Roosevelt, the first teddy bear was probably made by a German toymaker, Richard Steiff, at the beginning of this century. Steiff's bear soon became popular because, unlike earlier stuffed bears, its head and limbs were movable. The modern teddy shown here is a direct descendant of Steiff's prototype. It is made in six sections: a head, body, two arms, and two legs. For each section, pieces of golden-colored plush mohair are cut out, sewn together, and stuffed with wood wool. Felt forms the pads of the paws and feet. The eyes are made of colored plastic, and the nose and mouth are embroidered. Disks, screws, and washers connect the limbs and head to the body. When this teddy is tilted, it emits a bear-like growl.

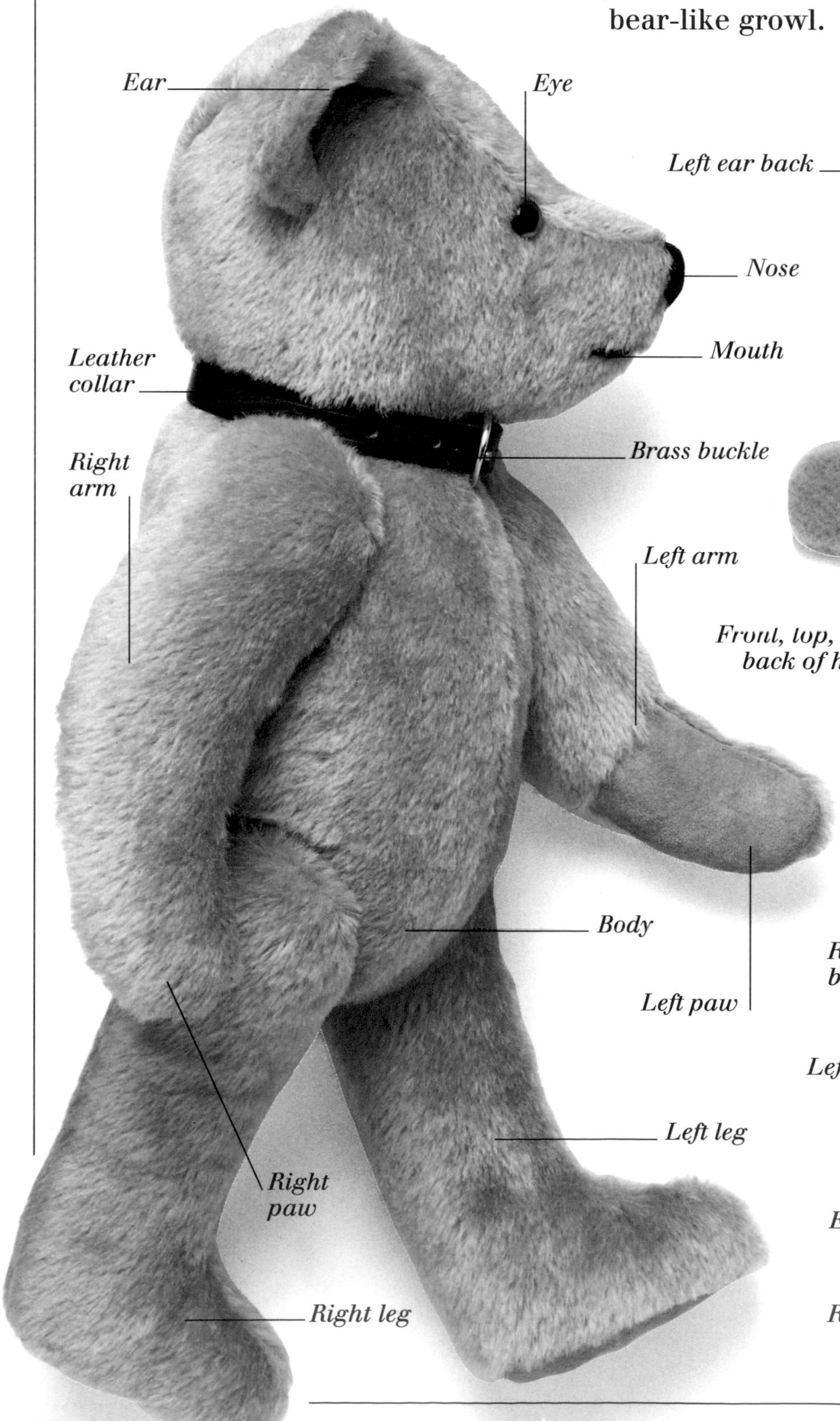

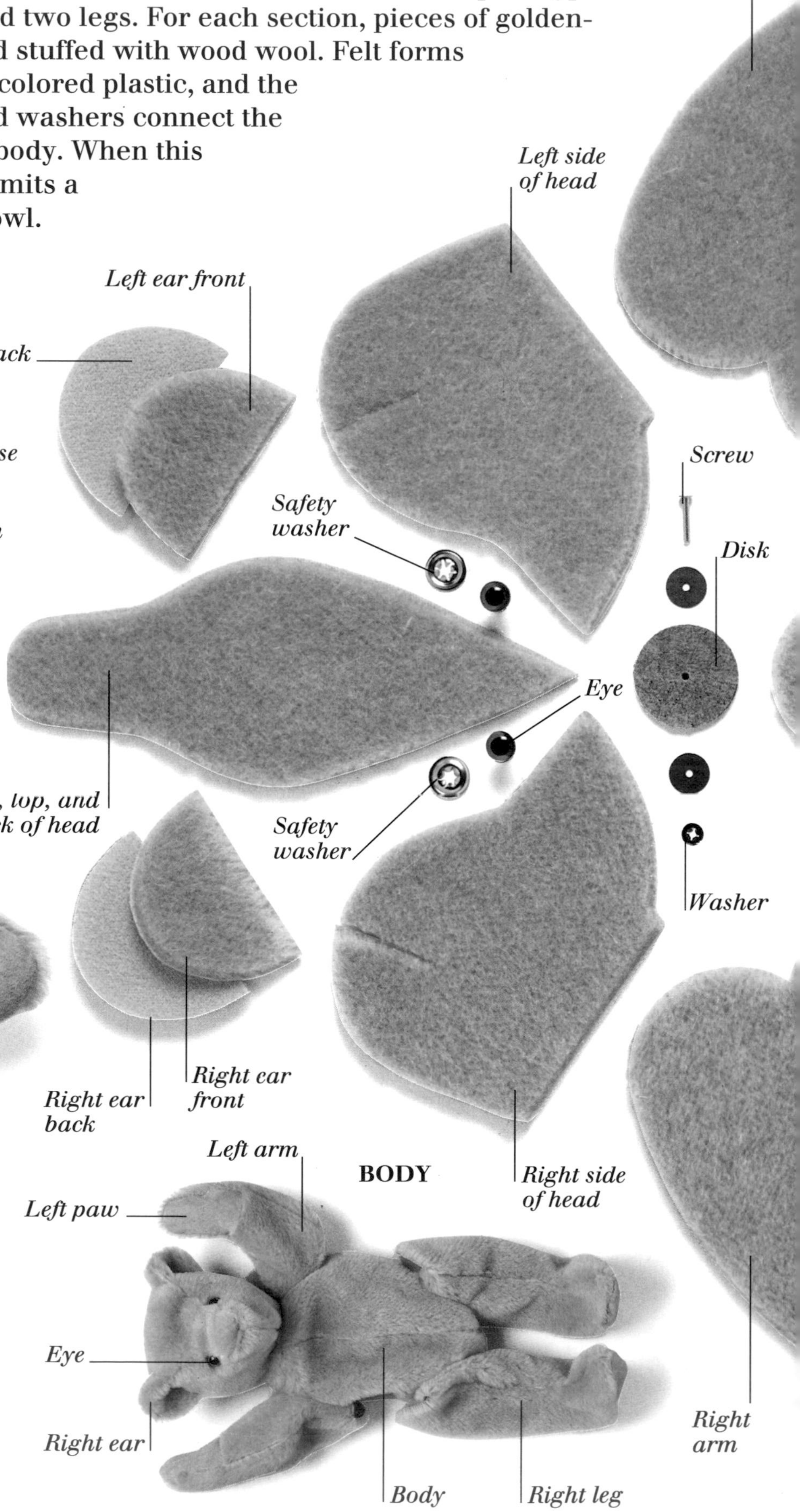

Ear

Eye

Nose

Mouth

Leather collar

Brass buckle

Right arm

Left arm

Body

Left paw

Right paw

Left leg

Right leg

Left arm

Left side of head

Left ear front

Left ear back

Screw

Safety washer

Disk

Eye

Front, top, and back of head

Safety washer

Eye

Washer

Right ear front

Right ear back

Left arm

Left paw

BODY

Right side of head

Eye

Right ear

Body

Right leg

Right arm

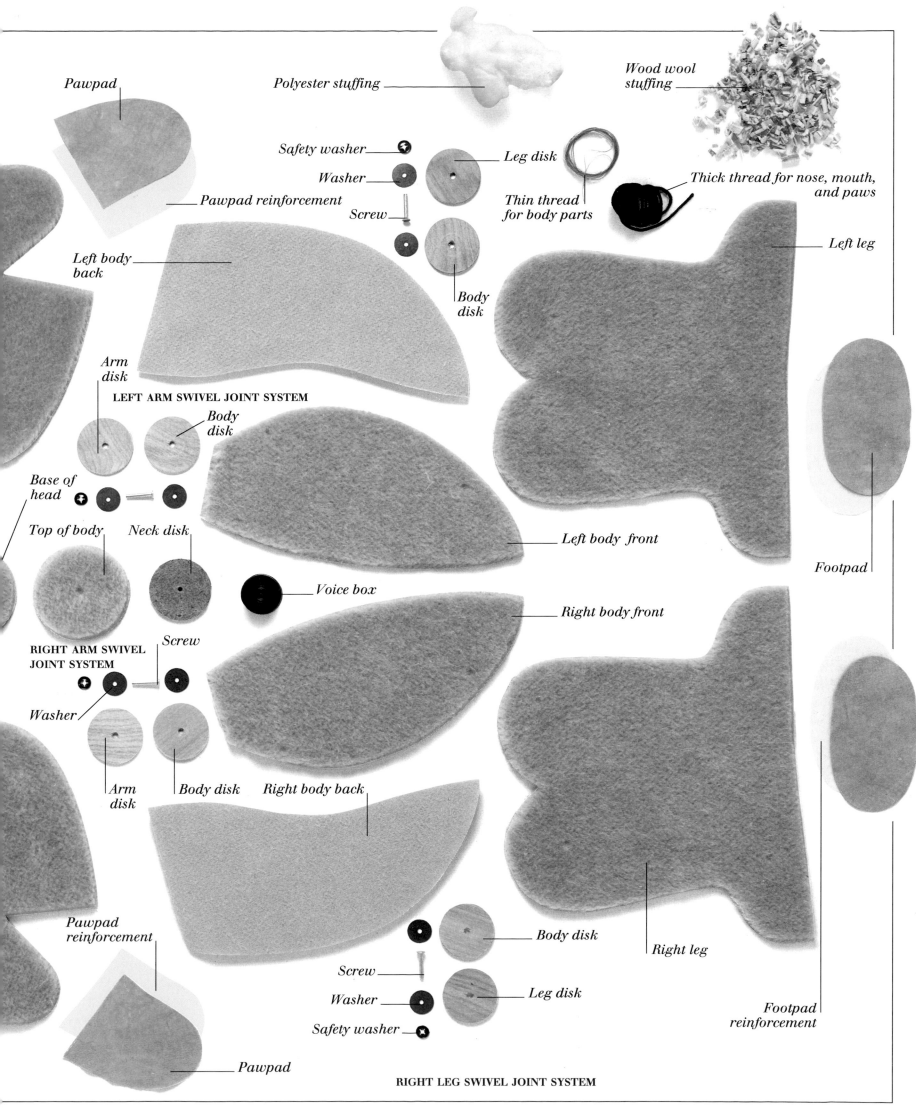

Pawpad

Polyester stuffing

Wood wool stuffing

Safety washer

Washer

Leg disk

Thin thread for body parts

Thick thread for nose, mouth, and paws

Pawpad reinforcement

Screw

Left leg

Left body back

Body disk

Arm disk

LEFT ARM SWIVEL JOINT SYSTEM

Body disk

Base of head

Top of body

Neck disk

Left body front

Voice box

Footpad

Right body front

RIGHT ARM SWIVEL JOINT SYSTEM

Screw

Washer

Arm disk

Body disk

Right body back

Right leg

Pawpad reinforcement

Body disk

Screw

Footpad reinforcement

Washer

Leg disk

Safety washer

Pawpad

RIGHT LEG SWIVEL JOINT SYSTEM

Lamp

THE FIRST SPRING-TENSIONED, adjustable work lamp was designed in 1934 by George Carwardine. This type of lamp imitates the human arm in the way that it can be kept in a fixed position or moved easily and precisely. In the arm, such control is achieved by coordinating the opposing action of paired muscles (e.g., when the biceps contracts, the triceps relaxes and the arm bends). In the work lamp, one muscle of a pair is represented by the springs that pull on the rigid bars of the lamp; the other muscle is represented by the nuts, bolts, screws, and washers in the lamp's joints that resist the pull of the springs. By balancing the pull of the springs against the resistance in the joints, the lamp's height and angle can be adjusted with minimal pressure.

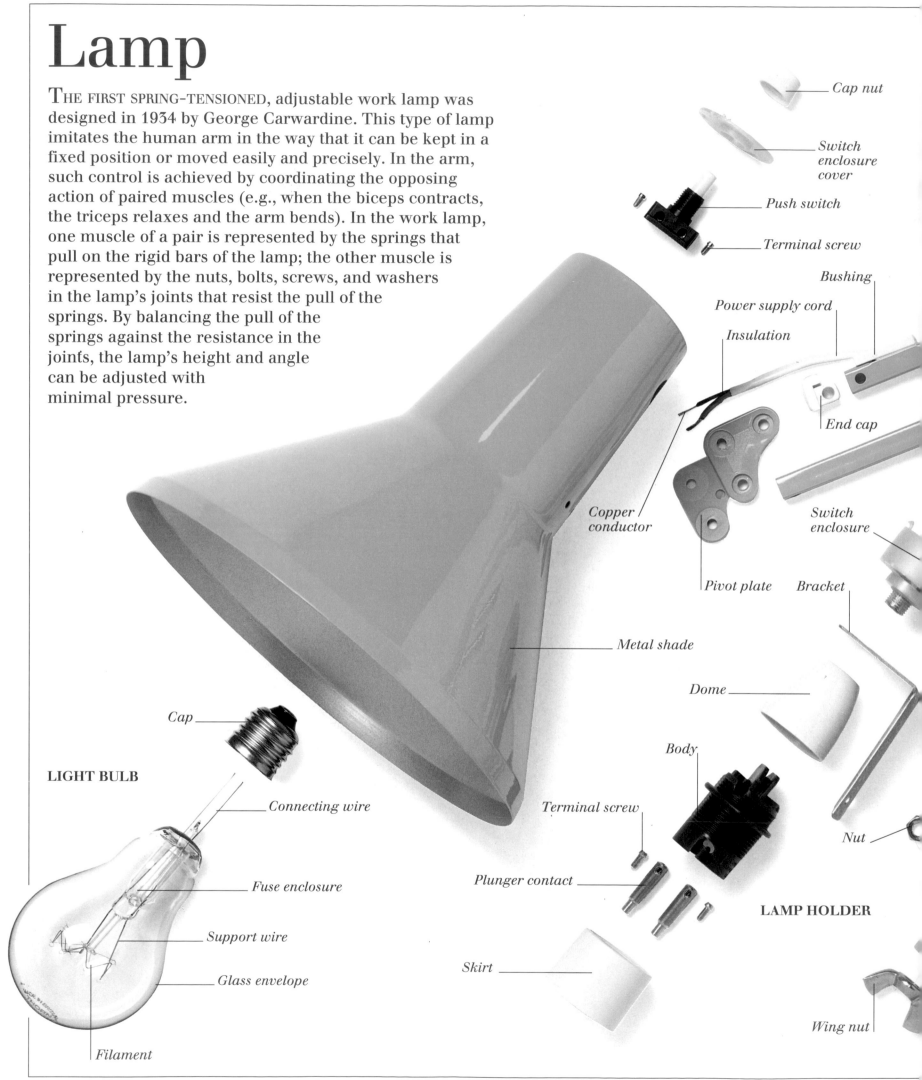

Cap nut

Switch enclosure cover

Push switch

Terminal screw

Bushing

Power supply cord

Insulation

End cap

Copper conductor

Switch enclosure

Pivot plate

Bracket

Metal shade

Dome

Body

Cap

LIGHT BULB

Connecting wire

Terminal screw

Nut

Fuse enclosure

Plunger contact

LAMP HOLDER

Support wire

Glass envelope

Skirt

Filament

Wing nut

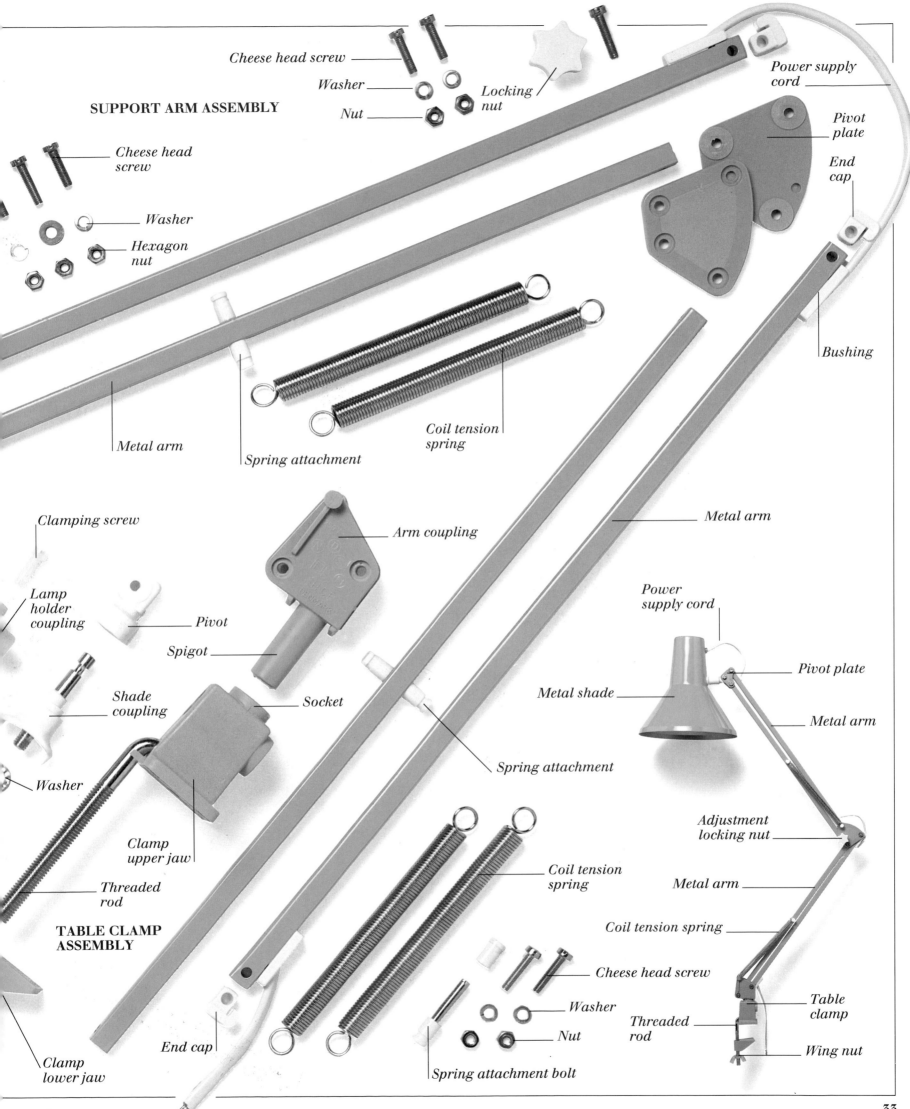

SUPPORT ARM ASSEMBLY

Cheese head screw

Washer

Nut

Locking nut

Cheese head screw

Washer

Hexagon nut

Metal arm

Spring attachment

Coil tension spring

Power supply cord

Pivot plate

End cap

Bushing

Metal arm

Clamping screw

Lamp holder coupling

Pivot

Spigot

Arm coupling

Power supply cord

Metal shade

Pivot plate

Metal arm

Shade coupling

Socket

Washer

Clamp upper jaw

Spring attachment

Adjustment locking nut

Threaded rod

Metal arm

TABLE CLAMP ASSEMBLY

Coil tension spring

Coil tension spring

Cheese head screw

Washer

Nut

End cap

Threaded rod

Table clamp

Clamp lower jaw

Spring attachment bolt

Wing nut

Chainsaw

A CHAINSAW IS A POWERFUL HAND-HELD tool for chopping wood, and for pruning or cutting down trees. It has a metal chain—similar to a bicycle chain—that moves around a guide bar. Attached to the links of the chain are teeth that cut the wood. Lubricating oil drips continually onto the chain to prevent it from sticking. Chainsaws can be powered by either a gasoline- or an electrically driven motor. The chainsaw shown here has a small gasoline-driven motor, which is started by a recoil rope rotor. This motor rotates a drive cog, or clutch sprocket, which turns the chain. Chainsaws have to perform in all weathers: in hot climates, a fanwheel cools the engine and for cold conditions some models have an electrically heated handle. This tool is potentially dangerous, but hand guards and a chain brake help protect the user from accidents.

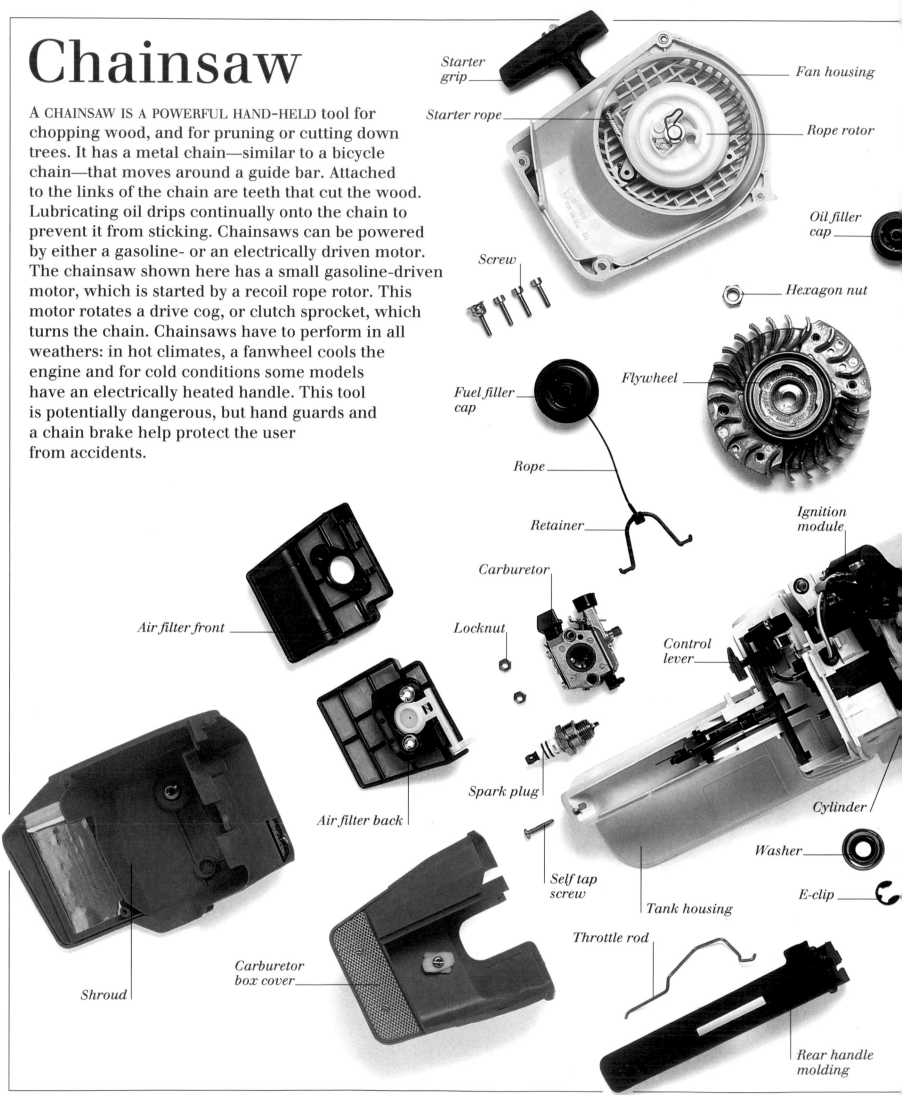

Starter grip

Starter rope

Fan housing

Rope rotor

Oil filler cap

Screw

Hexagon nut

Flywheel

Fuel filler cap

Rope

Retainer

Ignition module

Carburetor

Air filter front

Locknut

Control lever

Spark plug

Air filter back

Cylinder

Washer

Self tap screw

E-clip

Tank housing

Carburetor box cover

Throttle rod

Shroud

Rear handle molding

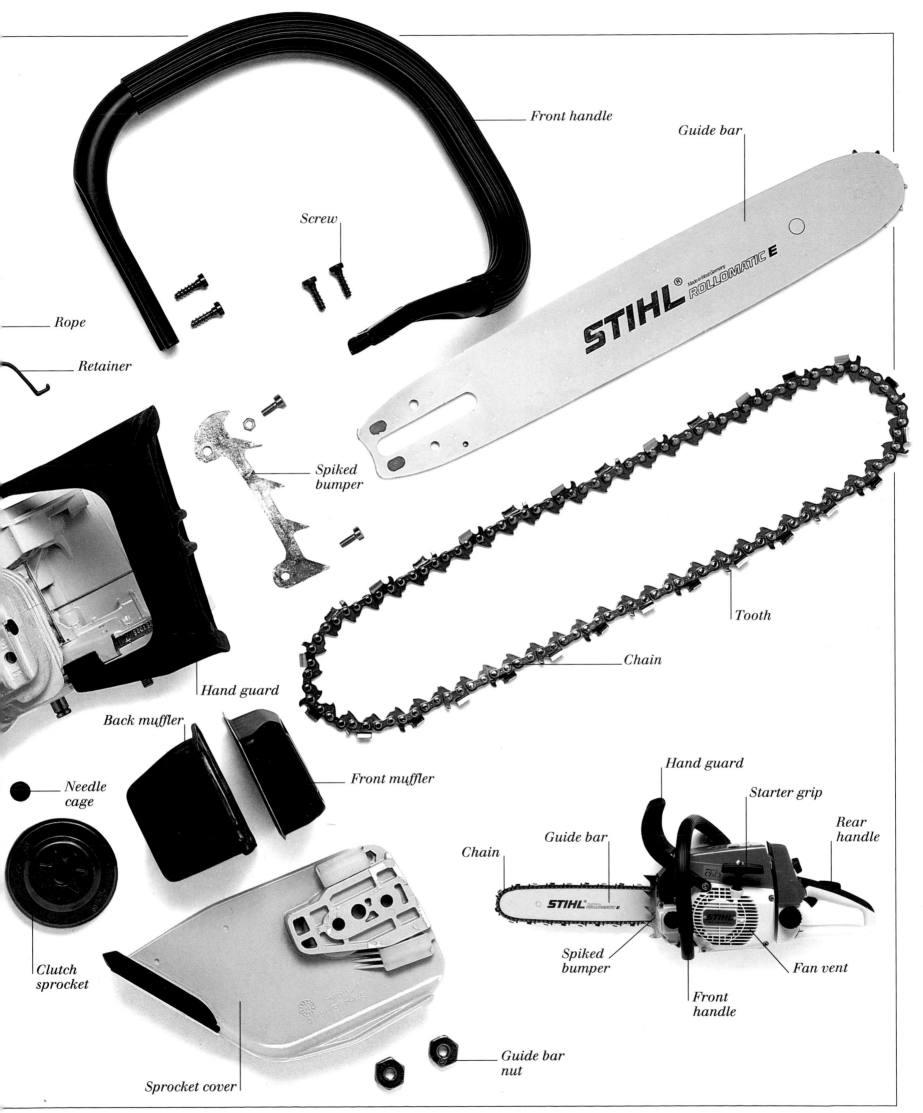

Front handle

Guide bar

Screw

Rope

Retainer

Spiked bumper

Hand guard

Back muffler

Front muffler

Needle cage

Clutch sprocket

Sprocket cover

Guide bar nut

Tooth

Chain

Hand guard

Starter grip

Guide bar

Rear handle

Chain

Spiked bumper

Front handle

Fan vent

STIHL® Made in West Germany ROLLOMATIC E

35

Mini television

MINIATURIZED TELEVISION SETS are small enough to be held in the hand while being watched. A signal sent by a broadcast transmitter is picked up by the television antenna and passed to an electron gun at the back of the television set. In response to the signal this gun produces an electron beam that is passed through a deflection yoke. The yoke contains magnets and coils that cause the beam to scan across the screen in a series of lines. The screen is coated with phosphor, which glows when hit by the beam. As the beam scans the screen, its strength is varied so that the phosphor glows with different intensities in different parts of the screen. A continuous sequence of 25 black-and-white pictures per second appears on the screen so rapidly that the illusion of a moving picture is created.

CATHODE RAY TUBE (CRT)

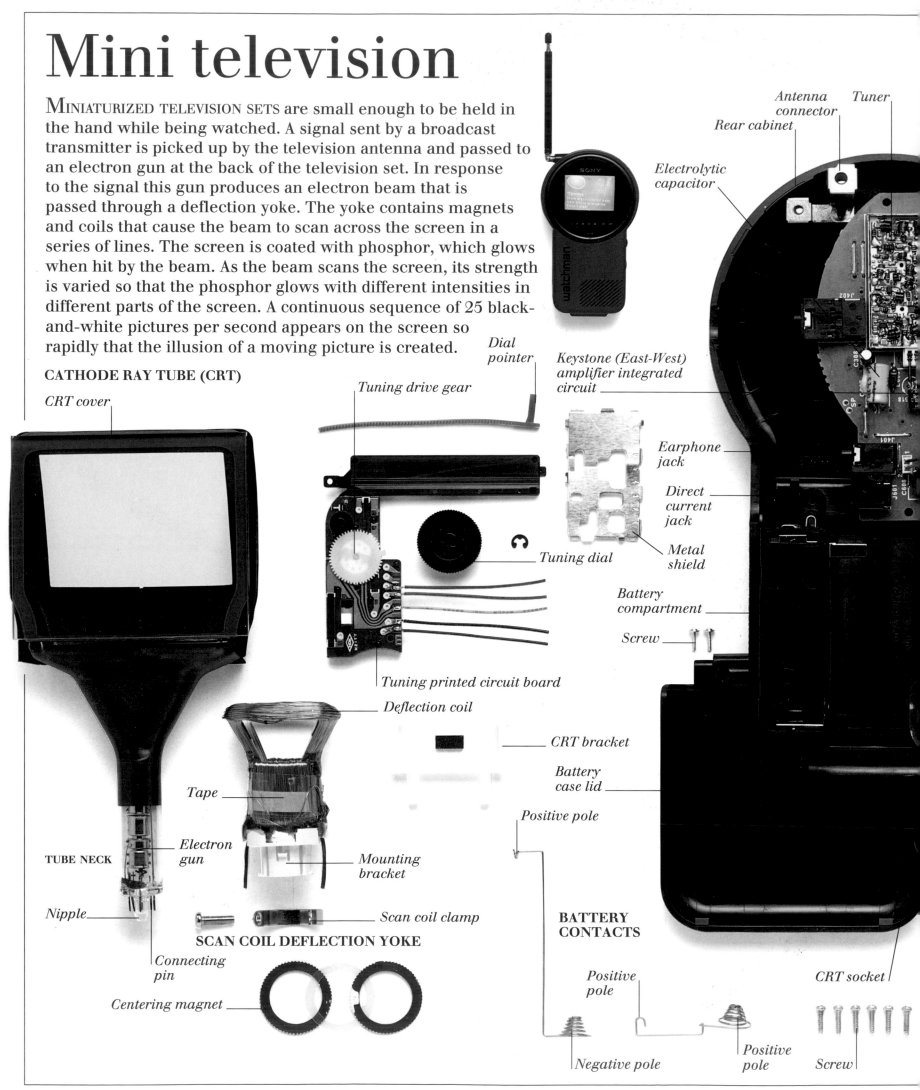

CRT cover

Dial pointer

Tuning drive gear

Keystone (East-West) amplifier integrated circuit

Rear cabinet

Antenna connector

Tuner

Electrolytic capacitor

Earphone jack

Direct current jack

Tuning dial

Metal shield

Battery compartment

Screw

Tuning printed circuit board

Deflection coil

CRT bracket

Tape

Battery case lid

Positive pole

TUBE NECK

Electron gun

Mounting bracket

Nipple

Scan coil clamp

BATTERY CONTACTS

SCAN COIL DEFLECTION YOKE

Connecting pin

Centering magnet

Positive pole

CRT socket

Negative pole

Positive pole

Screw

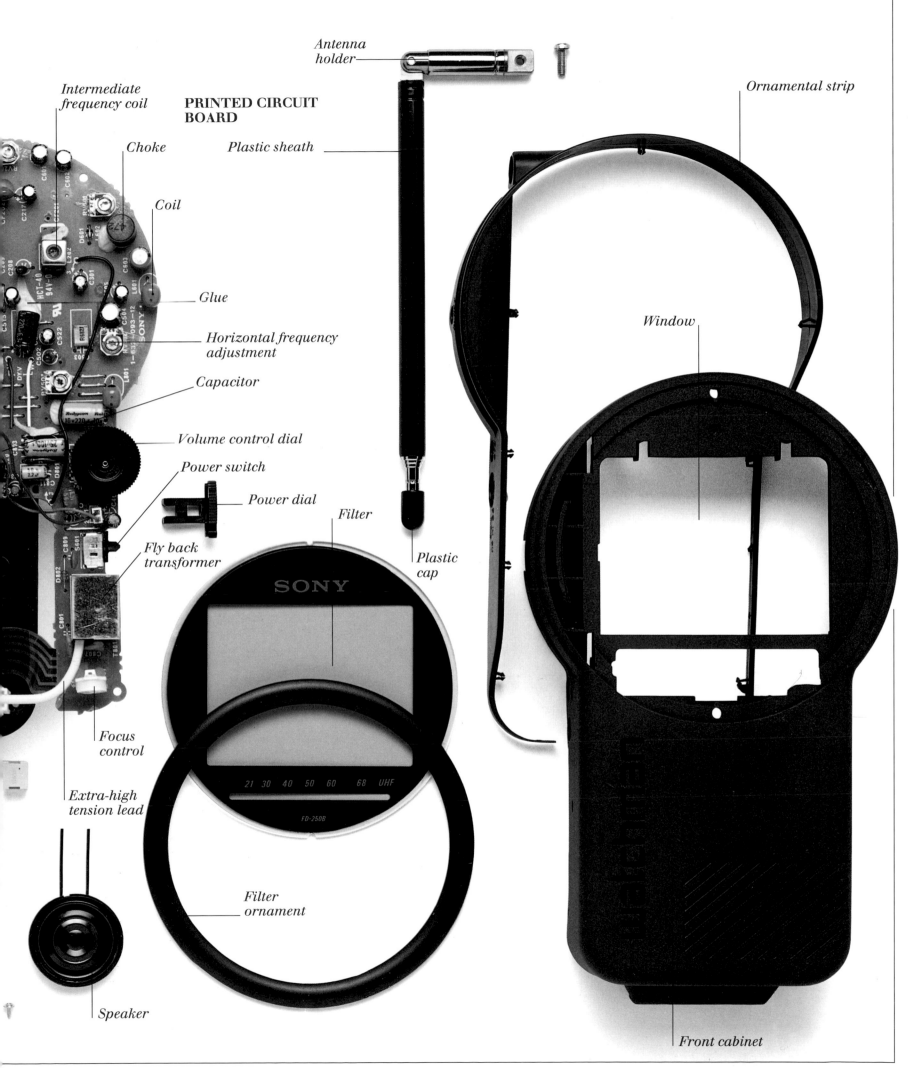

Intermediate
frequency coil

**PRINTED CIRCUIT
BOARD**

Choke

Coil

Glue

Horizontal frequency
adjustment

Capacitor

Volume control dial

Power switch

Power dial

Fly back
transformer

Focus
control

Extra-high
tension lead

Speaker

Antenna
holder

Plastic sheath

Filter

Plastic
cap

SONY

21 30 40 50 60 68 UHF

FD-250B

Filter
ornament

Ornamental strip

Window

Front cabinet

Chair

A TRADITIONALLY MADE DINING CHAIR, such as the Regency-style carver shown here, is held together, not by nails or bolts, but by snugly fitting joints, screws, dowels, and glue. Its curved arms and top splats, as well as its tapering legs, are cut from seasoned—that is, dried—mahogany. Mortice slots in the back legs receive the tenon tongues of the top and bottom splats; angled grooves at the top of the back legs, called rebates, take the curved arm rail. Though the various joints are so tight-fitting that they could produce a solid frame on their own, screws and glue are used to give the joints added strength. The comfortable, upholstered seatpad shown here consists of a patterned cover, calico lining, and foam padding that has been treated for fire safety; it is supported by webbing stretched across a wood frame.

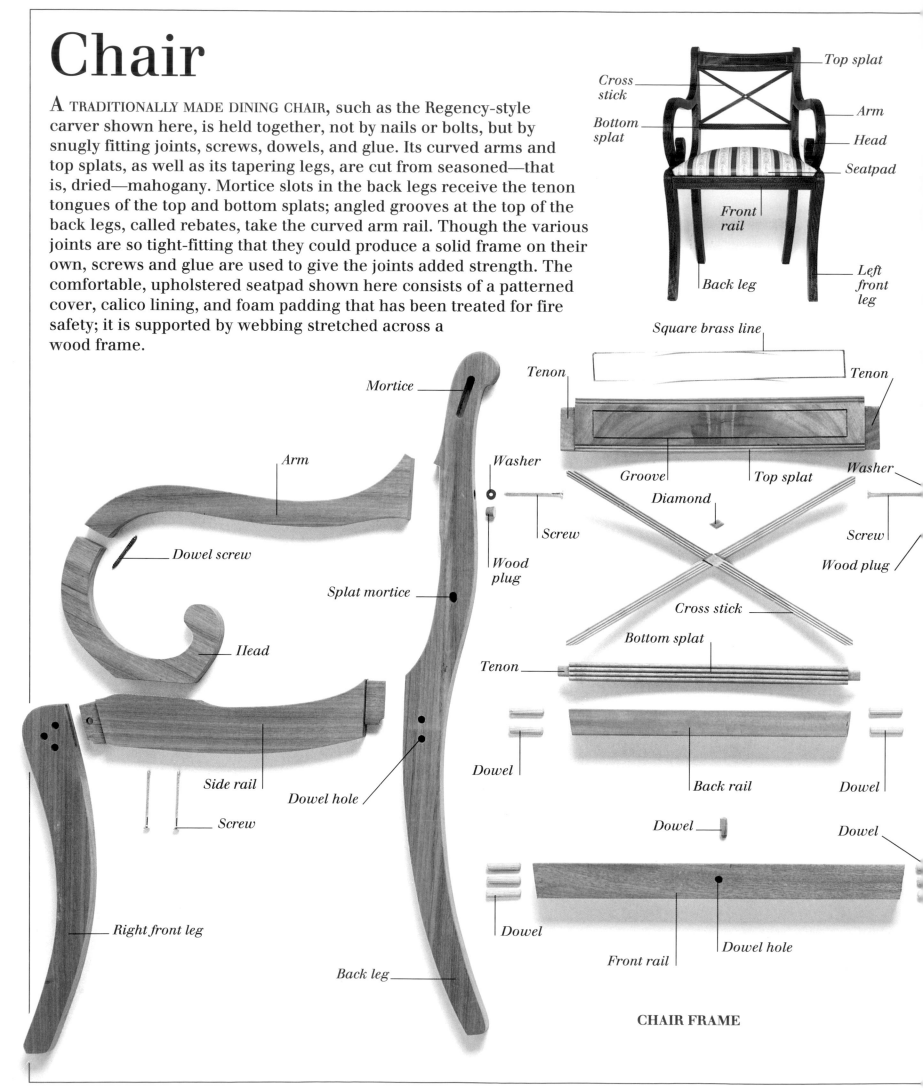

Cross stick

Top splat

Bottom splat

Arm

Head

Seatpad

Front rail

Back leg

Left front leg

Mortice

Arm

Dowel screw

Head

Right front leg

Splat mortice

Washer

Screw

Wood plug

Side rail

Dowel hole

Screw

Back leg

Tenon

Square brass line

Tenon

Groove

Top splat

Diamond

Washer

Screw

Wood plug

Cross stick

Bottom splat

Tenon

Dowel

Back rail

Dowel

Dowel

Dowel

Front rail

Dowel hole

Dowel

CHAIR FRAME

SEAT UPHOLSTERY

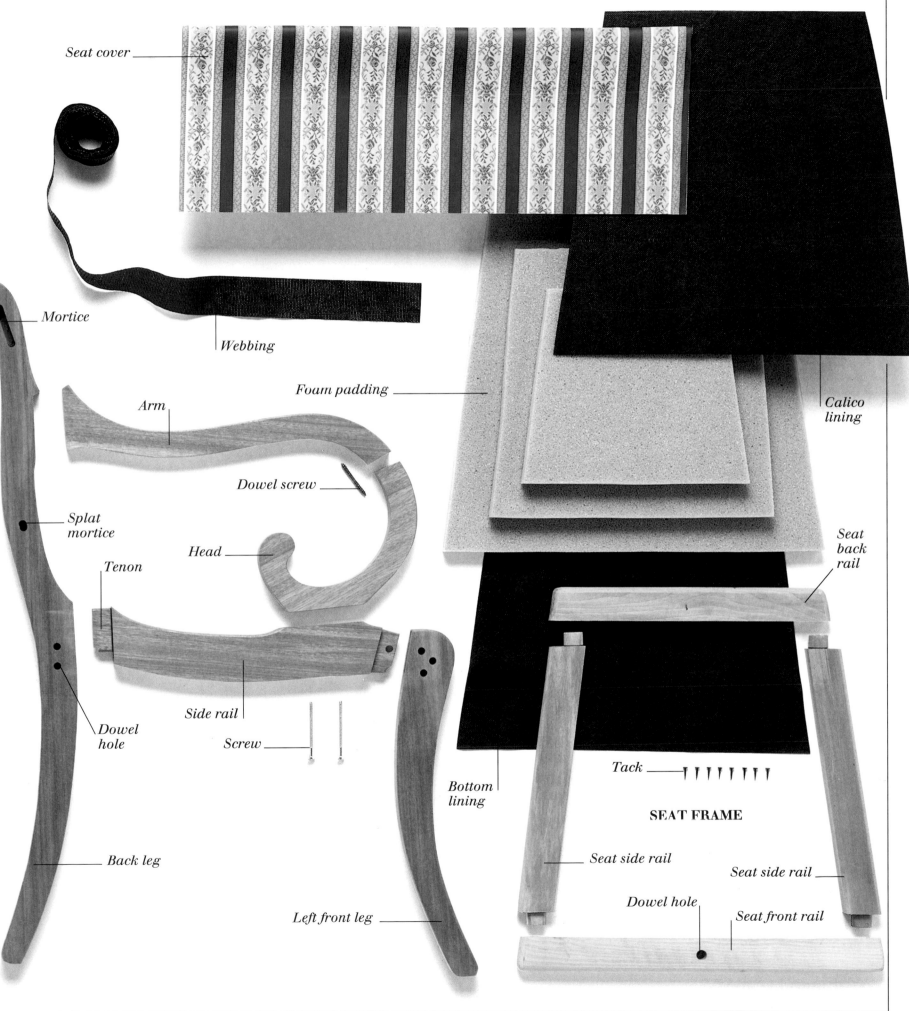

Seat cover

Mortice

Webbing

Arm

Foam padding

Calico lining

Dowel screw

Splat mortice

Head

Tenon

Seat back rail

Side rail

Screw

Bottom lining

Tack

Back leg

SEAT FRAME

Dowel hole

Seat side rail

Left front leg

Seat side rail

Dowel hole

Seat front rail

Food processor

A FOOD PROCESSOR MAKES QUICK WORK of preparing ingredients. Razor-sharp blades of different shapes cut, chop, shred, slice, grate, or mince while other attachments whisk, knead, mix, or juice. The machine is powered by an electric motor that turns a drive wheel connected to a drive belt. This belt rotates a drive shaft gear that spins a drive shaft at high speed. The drive shaft then turns the attachment that is mounted on it. Because the spinning blades are potentially dangerous, safety is an important feature of all food processors. Safety interlocks make it impossible to operate the machine unless the lid is securely fixed. The cook also cannot reach the blades when the machine is working and so must drop ingredients through the filling funnel or into the rotating tray of a wide feed tube.

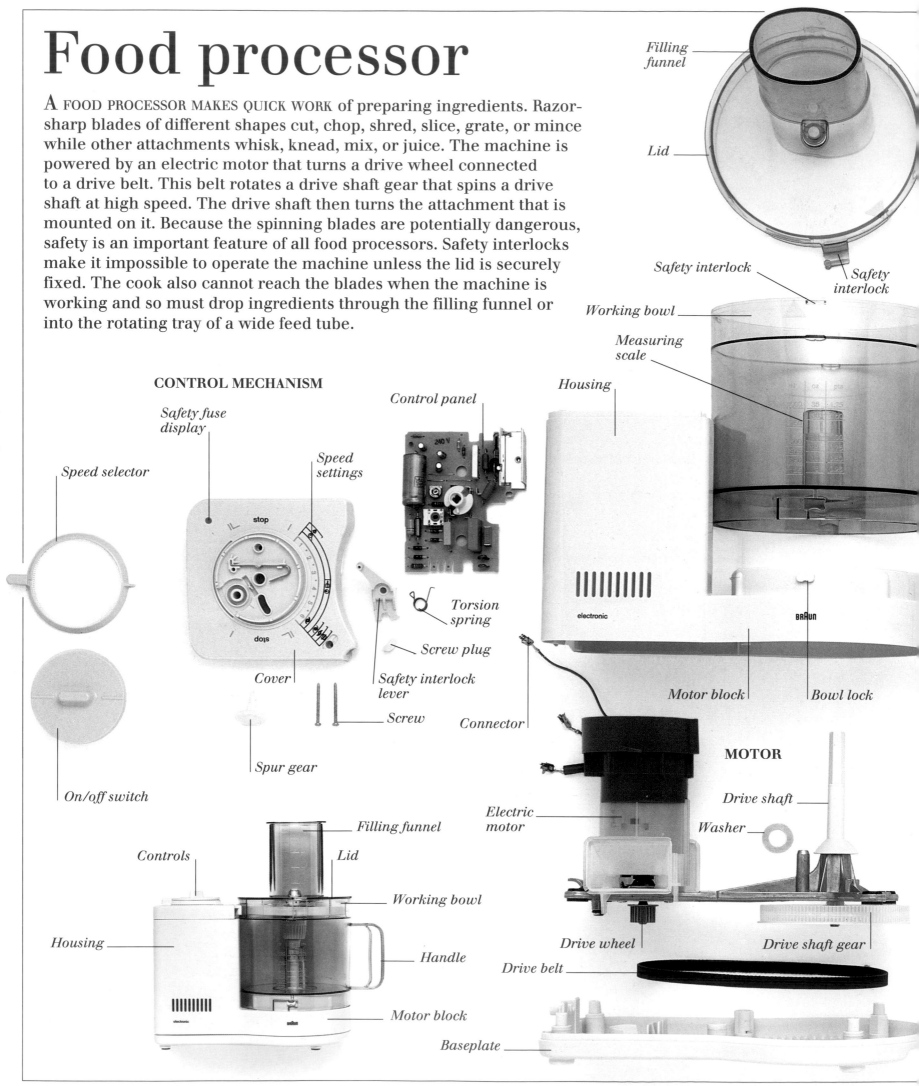

Filling funnel

Lid

Safety interlock

Safety interlock

Working bowl

Measuring scale

Housing

CONTROL MECHANISM

Safety fuse display

Speed selector

Speed settings

Control panel

stop

240 V

stop

Torsion spring

Screw plug

Cover

Safety interlock lever

Spur gear

Screw

Connector

On/off switch

Motor block

Bowl lock

electronic

BRAUN

MOTOR

Drive shaft

Electric motor

Washer

Controls

Filling funnel

Lid

Working bowl

Housing

Handle

Drive wheel

Drive shaft gear

Drive belt

electronic

braun

Motor block

Baseplate

40

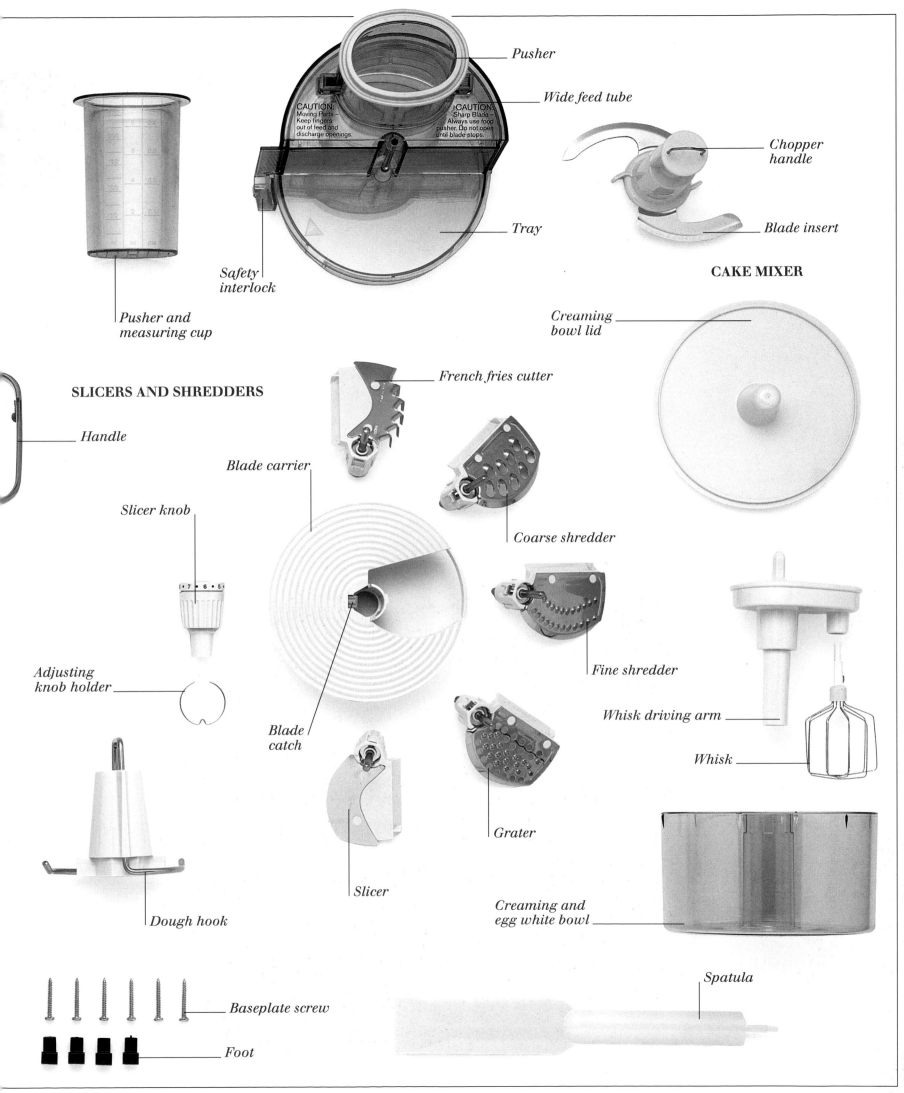

Pusher

Wide feed tube

CAUTION:
Moving Parts –
Keep fingers
out of feed and
discharge openings.

CAUTION:
Sharp Blade –
Always use food
pusher. Do not open
until blade stops.

Chopper handle

Tray

Blade insert

Safety interlock

CAKE MIXER

Pusher and measuring cup

Creaming bowl lid

SLICERS AND SHREDDERS

French fries cutter

Handle

Blade carrier

Coarse shredder

Slicer knob

Fine shredder

Adjusting knob holder

Whisk driving arm

Blade catch

Whisk

Grater

Dough hook

Slicer

Creaming and egg white bowl

Spatula

Baseplate screw

Foot

Typewriter

A TYPEWRITER IS A HAND-OPERATED printing machine. It has a set of keys marked with letters, figures, and other symbols. When the typist strikes a key with a finger, a system of levers or an electronic signal moves a raised version of the symbol, the type, toward an inked ribbon. The type may be on a series of bars or may be arranged around a sphere called a "golf ball." As the type makes contact, it prints an image of itself onto a sheet of paper held in position on the platen. A spring then moves the carriage and the paper forward a space. The next symbol can then be typed beside the first one.

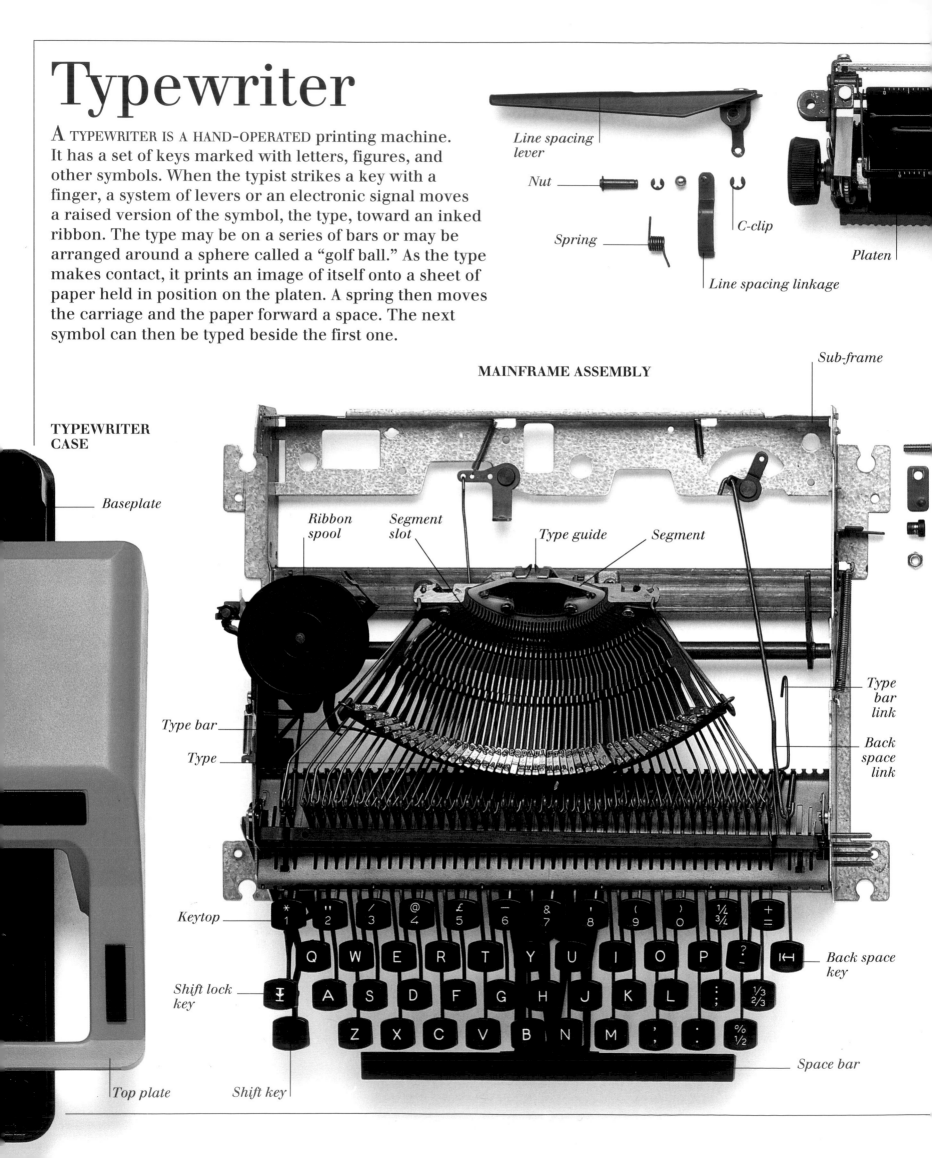

Line spacing lever

Nut

Spring

C-clip

Line spacing linkage

Platen

Sub-frame

MAINFRAME ASSEMBLY

TYPEWRITER CASE

Baseplate

Ribbon spool

Segment slot

Type guide

Segment

Type bar link

Back space link

Type bar

Type

Keytop

Back space key

Shift lock key

Top plate

Shift key

Space bar

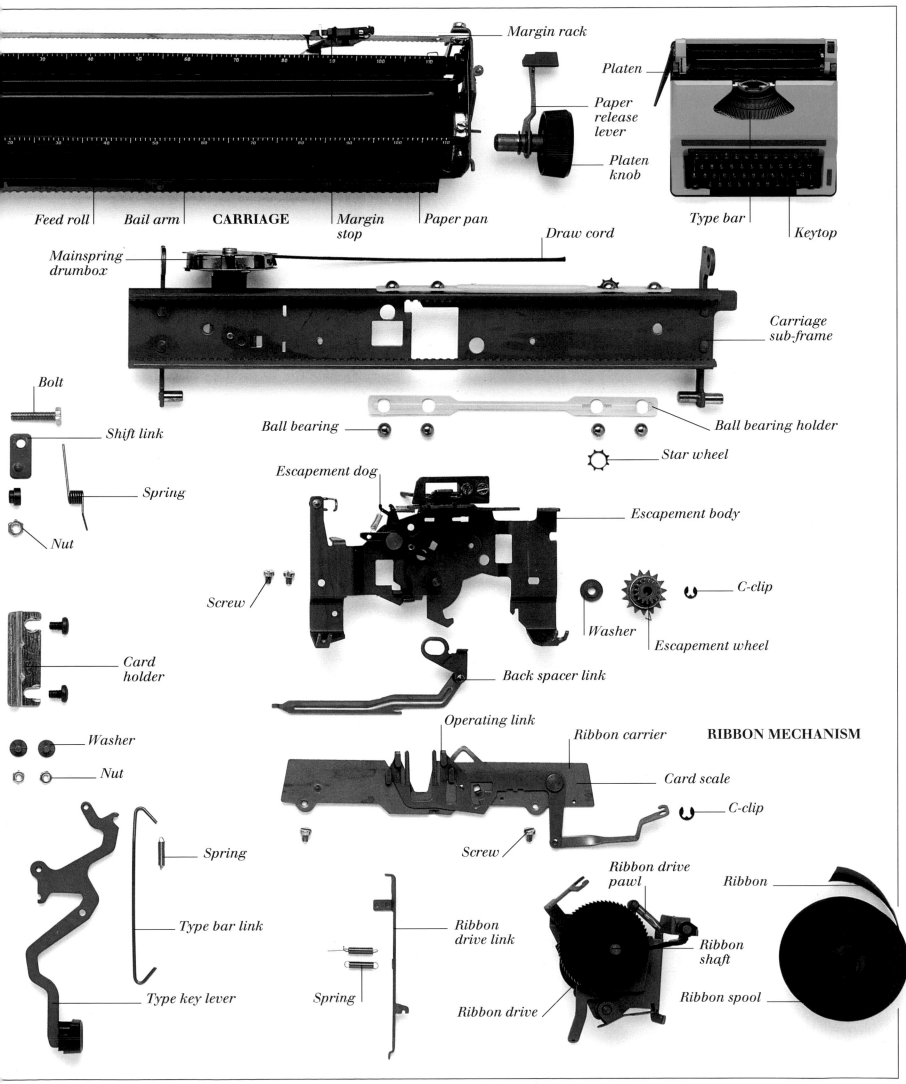

Margin rack

Platen

Paper release lever

Platen knob

Feed roll   Bail arm   **CARRIAGE**   Margin stop   Paper pan

Type bar

Keytop

Mainspring drumbox

Draw cord

Carriage sub-frame

Bolt

Shift link

Ball bearing

Ball bearing holder

Spring

Star wheel

Nut

Escapement dog

Escapement body

Screw

C-clip

Card holder

Washer

Escapement wheel

Back spacer link

Washer

Operating link

Ribbon carrier

RIBBON MECHANISM

Nut

Card scale

Spring

C-clip

Type bar link

Screw

Ribbon drive pawl

Ribbon

Type key lever

Ribbon drive link

Spring

Ribbon drive

Ribbon shaft

Ribbon spool

Suitcase

In the 19th century, wealthy people travelled abroad, they took their belongings in a series of specialized containers. Hats were in hatboxes, books and shoes and other general items were packed in trunks, and smart clothes for men were packed in flat valises, or suitcases. During this century, the flat suitcase has become the all-purpose travel bag, and good suitcases are designed to cope with all the potential problems of a long journey. The ideal suitcase has pockets for storing items such as shoes, and protects its contents from water, heat, humidity, sand, animals, and thieves.

Washer

Screw

Top corner piece

SUITCASE BODY

Trim patch

Wire frame

Metal fitting

Handle trim

Hardware buckle

Metal slider

Padlock

Webbing

Logo

Logo patch

Metal slider

Handle

Key

Retractable pull-handle

Webbing

Metal fitting

Hardware buckle

Handle trim

Trim patch

Body side

Body

Logo patch

Logo

Trim patch

Name tag

Top corner piece

Webbing

Body side

Webbing

Handle

Name tag

Hardware buckle

Screw

Washer

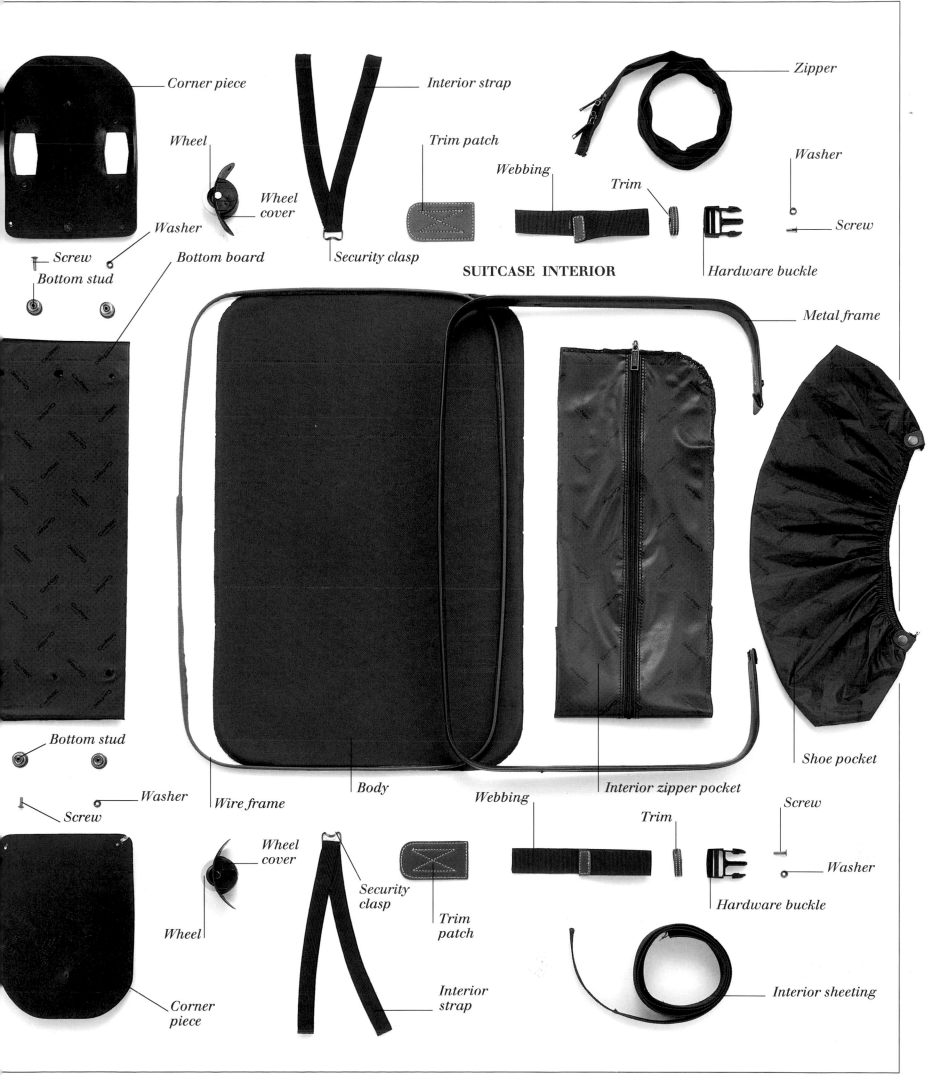

Corner piece

Wheel

Wheel cover

Washer

Screw

Bottom stud

Bottom board

Interior strap

Security clasp

Trim patch

Webbing

Trim

Zipper

Washer

Screw

Hardware buckle

SUITCASE INTERIOR

Metal frame

Bottom stud

Washer

Screw

Wire frame

Body

Webbing

Interior zipper pocket

Shoe pocket

Wheel cover

Security clasp

Trim patch

Trim

Screw

Washer

Hardware buckle

Wheel

Corner piece

Interior strap

Interior sheeting

Toaster

MOST ELECTRIC TOASTERS NOT ONLY GRILL slices of bread, they also pop them up when ready. While the slices rest on a spring-loaded rack, electric heating elements toast the bread. At the same time, a bimetallic strip heats and expands. One of the two metals in this strip expands more quickly than the other, causing the strip to curve. As it bends, it completes an electrical circuit and activates an electromagnet. The magnet attracts a catch, releasing the spring that holds the rack down in the toaster. The elements switch off, and the toasted slices pop up.

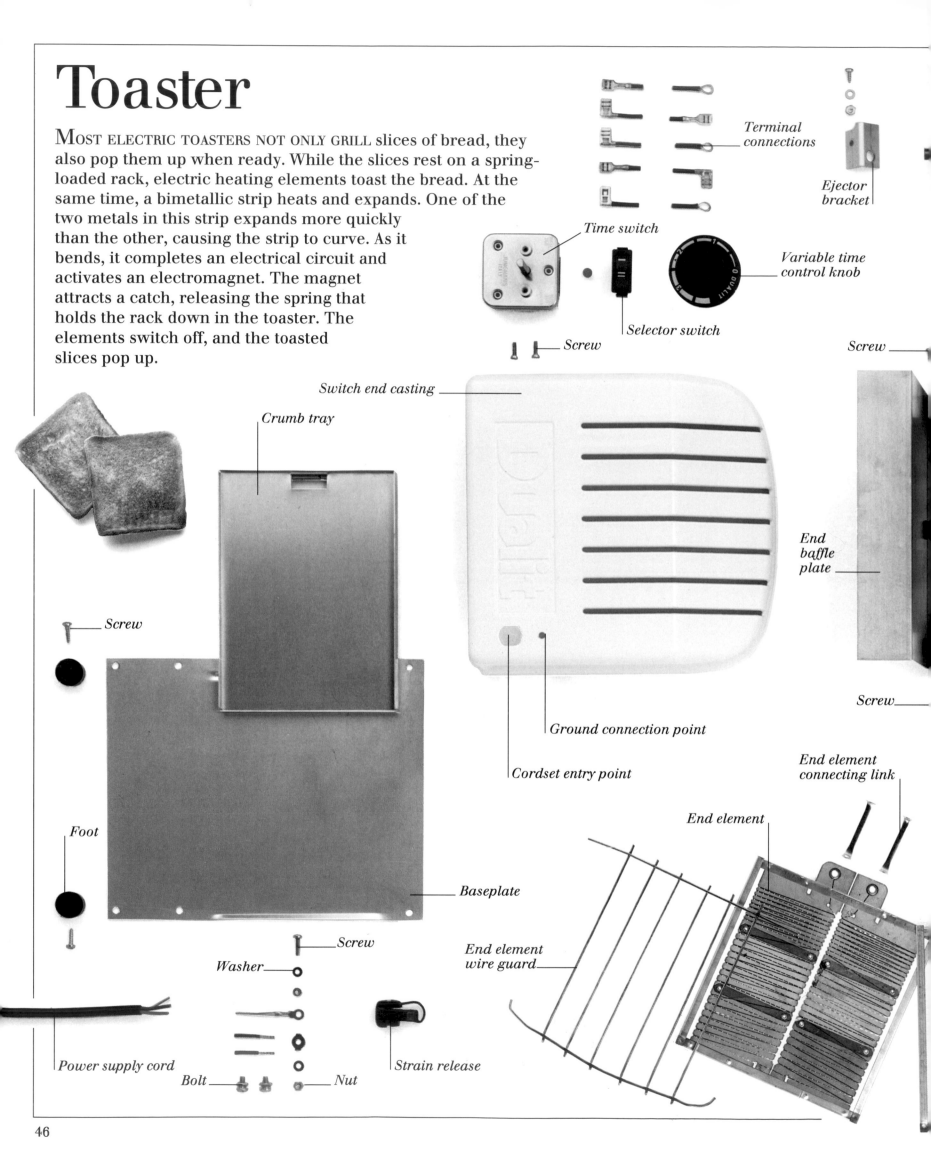

Terminal connections

Ejector bracket

Time switch

Variable time control knob

Selector switch

Screw

Screw

Switch end casting

Crumb tray

End baffle plate

Screw

Screw

Ground connection point

Foot

Cordset entry point

End element connecting link

End element

Baseplate

End element wire guard

Screw

Washer

Power supply cord

Strain release

Bolt

Nut

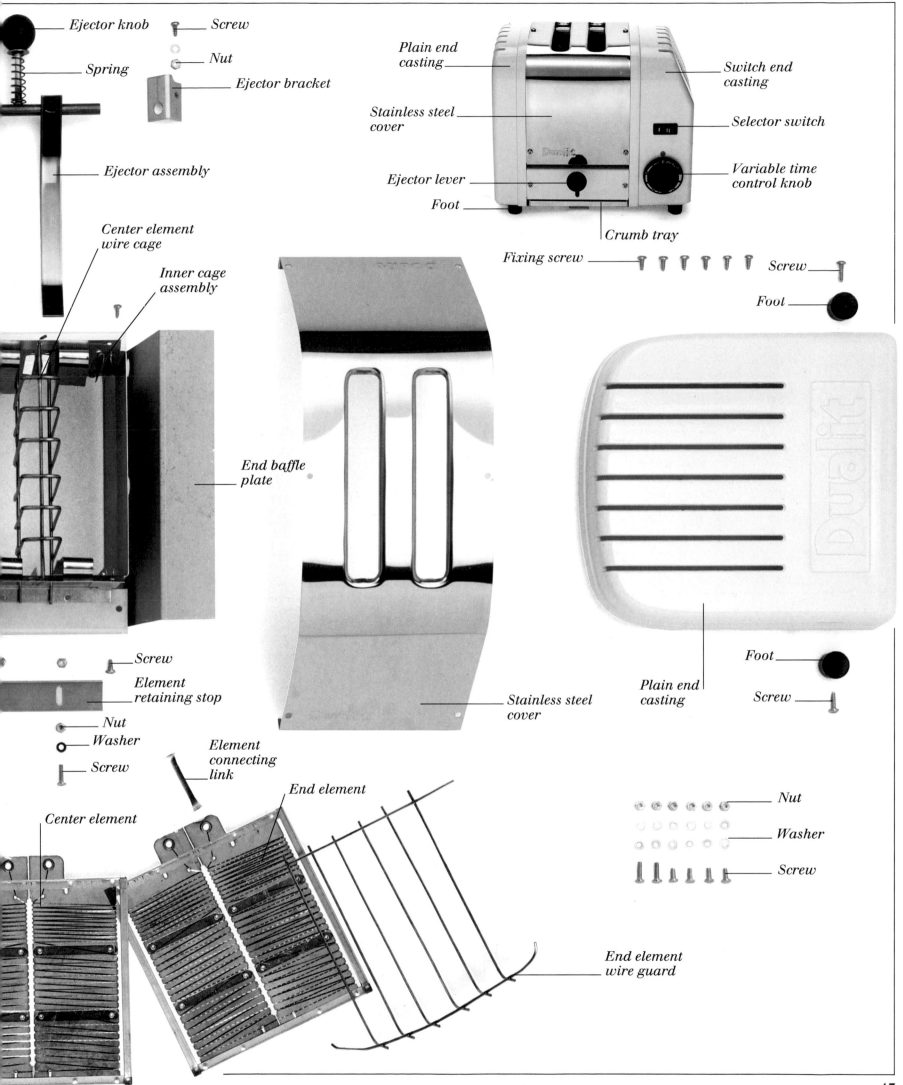

Ejector knob

Screw

Nut

Spring

Ejector bracket

Ejector assembly

Plain end casting

Switch end casting

Stainless steel cover

Selector switch

Ejector lever

Variable time control knob

Foot

Crumb tray

Center element wire cage

Fixing screw

Screw

Inner cage assembly

Foot

End baffle plate

Screw

Element retaining stop

Foot

Nut

Plain end casting

Washer

Stainless steel cover

Screw

Screw

Element connecting link

Nut

Center element

End element

Washer

Screw

End element wire guard

Umbrellas

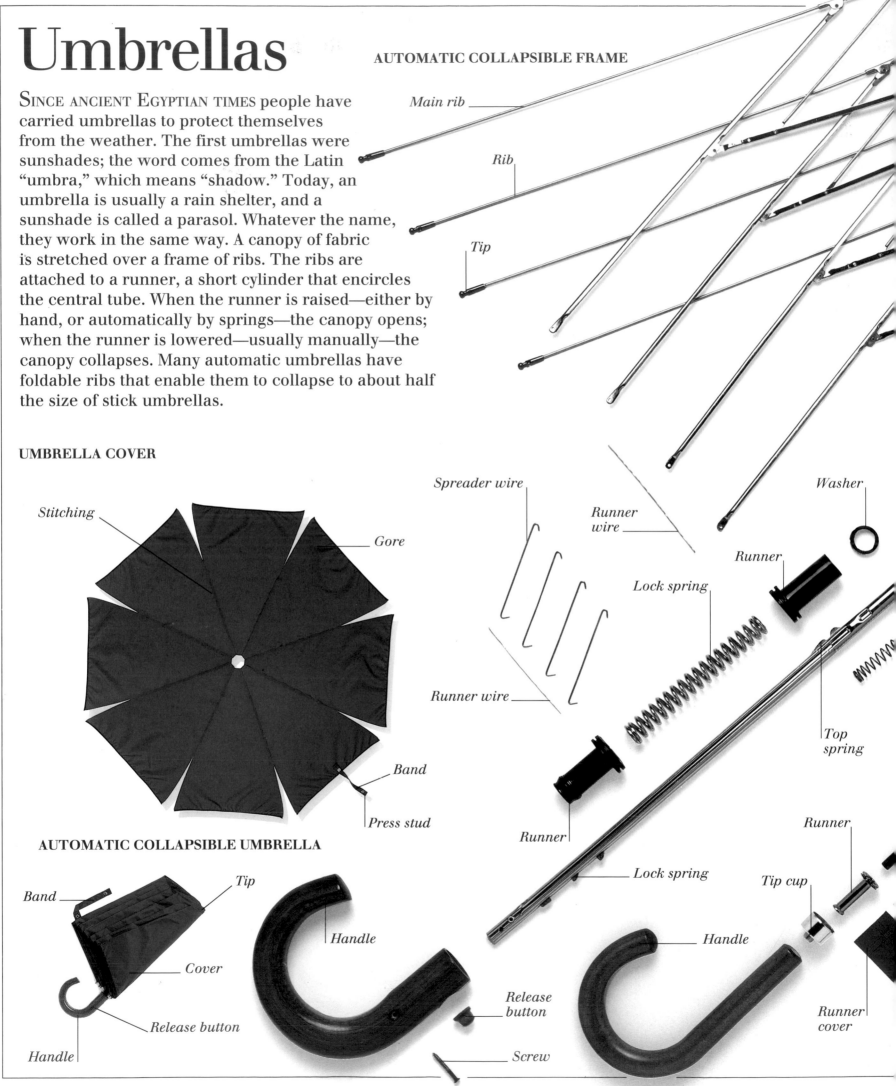

Since ancient Egyptian times people have carried umbrellas to protect themselves from the weather. The first umbrellas were sunshades; the word comes from the Latin "umbra," which means "shadow." Today, an umbrella is usually a rain shelter, and a sunshade is called a parasol. Whatever the name, they work in the same way. A canopy of fabric is stretched over a frame of ribs. The ribs are attached to a runner, a short cylinder that encircles the central tube. When the runner is raised—either by hand, or automatically by springs—the canopy opens; when the runner is lowered—usually manually—the canopy collapses. Many automatic umbrellas have foldable ribs that enable them to collapse to about half the size of stick umbrellas.

AUTOMATIC COLLAPSIBLE FRAME

Main rib

Rib

Tip

UMBRELLA COVER

Stitching

Gore

Spreader wire

Runner wire

Washer

Runner

Lock spring

Runner wire

Top spring

Band

Press stud

Runner

Lock spring

Runner

AUTOMATIC COLLAPSIBLE UMBRELLA

Band

Tip

Handle

Tip cup

Handle

Band

Cover

Release button

Runner cover

Release button

Handle

Screw

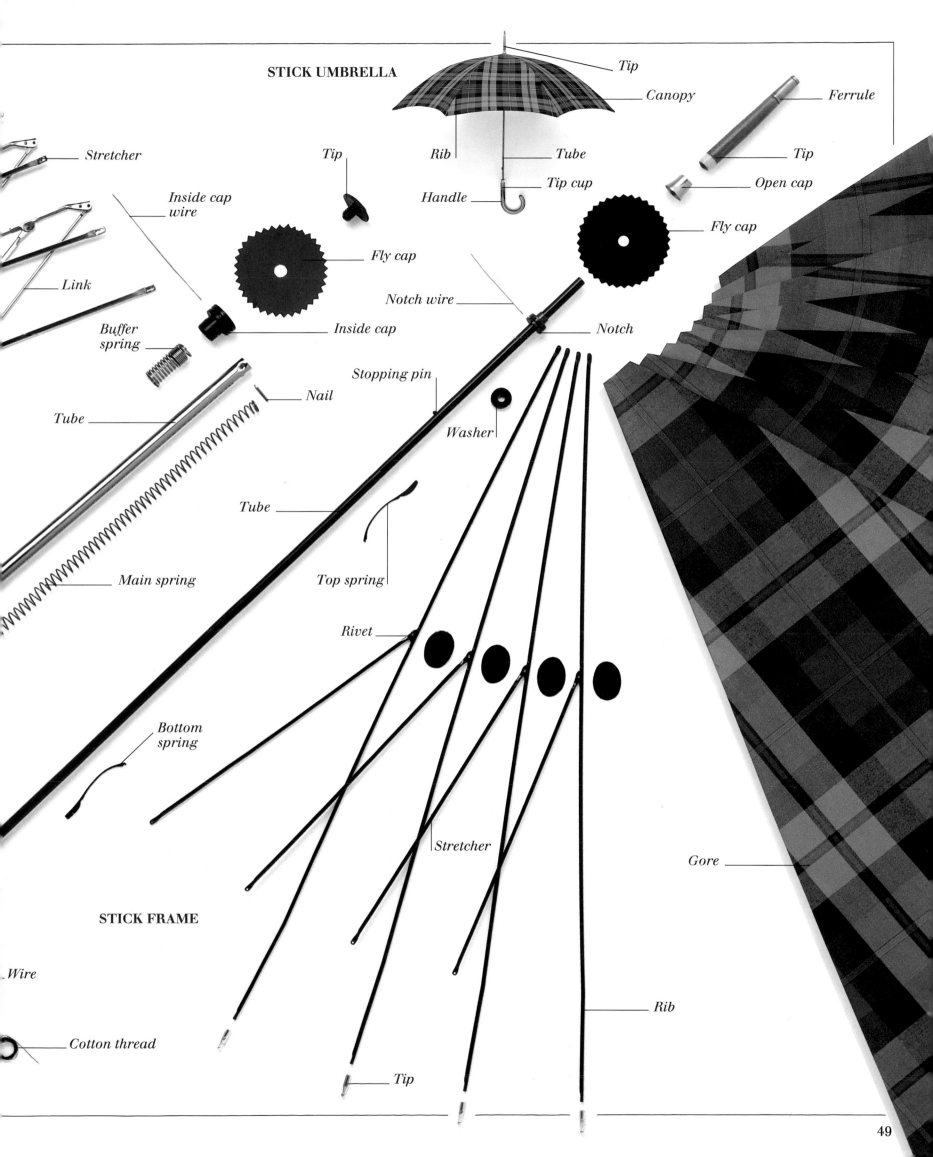

STICK UMBRELLA

Tip

Canopy

Ferrule

Rib

Tube

Tip

Handle

Tip cup

Open cap

Stretcher

Fly cap

Inside cap
wire

Tip

Fly cap

Link

Notch wire

Buffer
spring

Inside cap

Notch

Stopping pin

Tube

Washer

Nail

Tube

Top spring

Main spring

Rivet

Bottom
spring

Stretcher

Gore

STICK FRAME

Wire

Rib

Cotton thread

Tip

Lawnmower

THE SHARP BLADES OF A LAWNMOWER—whether driven by electrical, gasoline, or human power—shave grass close to the ground. The gasoline-powered type shown here has a small engine that is electrically ignited by a battery and spark plug. This engine rotates a horizontal blade at the base of the lawnmower, which then slices the grass against a fixed blade. A grass bag at the back of the machine collects the cuttings. As the engine rotates the blades, it also turns the rear wheels, moving the lawnmower forward. Gears ensure that the horizontal blade spins faster than the wheels so that all of the grass is cut neatly before the lawnmower moves on.

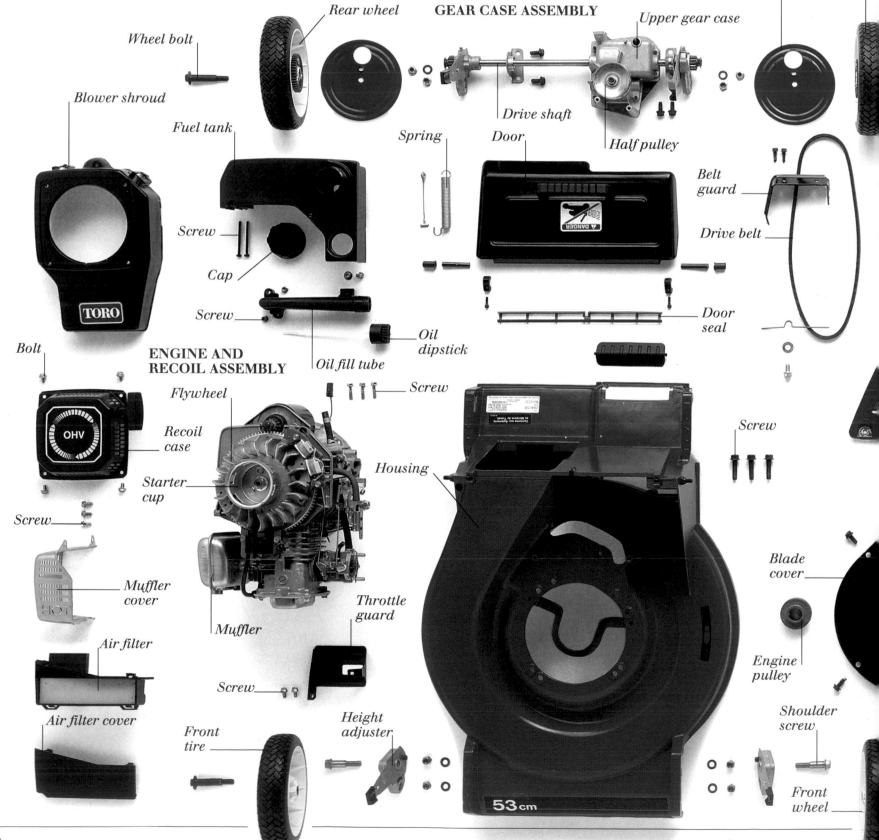

Rear tire

Wheel cover

Rear wheel

GEAR CASE ASSEMBLY

Upper gear case

Wheel bolt

Blower shroud

Fuel tank

Drive shaft

Half pulley

Spring

Door

Belt guard

Drive belt

Screw

Cap

Screw

Door seal

Oil dipstick

Bolt

ENGINE AND RECOIL ASSEMBLY

Oil fill tube

Screw

OHV

Flywheel

Recoil case

Screw

Starter cup

Housing

Screw

Screw

Muffler cover

Blade cover

Air filter

Throttle guard

Muffler

Engine pulley

Air filter cover

Screw

Front tire

Height adjuster

Shoulder screw

Front wheel

53cm

50

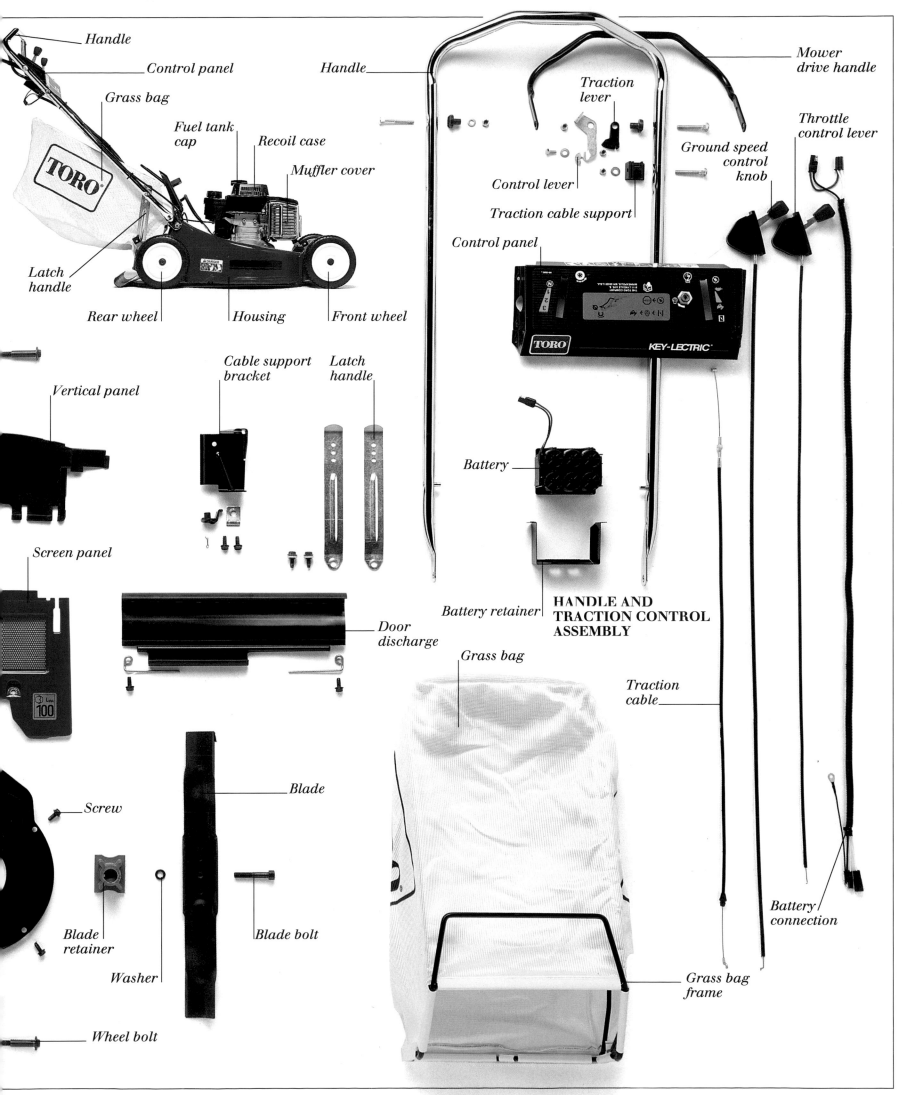

Handle

Control panel

Grass bag

Fuel tank cap

Recoil case

Muffler cover

Latch handle

Rear wheel

Housing

Front wheel

Handle

Mower drive handle

Traction lever

Throttle control lever

Ground speed control knob

Control lever

Traction cable support

Control panel

Vertical panel

Cable support bracket

Latch handle

Battery

Screen panel

Door discharge

Battery retainer

HANDLE AND TRACTION CONTROL ASSEMBLY

Grass bag

Traction cable

Blade

Screw

Blade retainer

Washer

Blade bolt

Battery connection

Grass bag frame

Wheel bolt

51

Saddle

THE FIRST HORSEBACK RIDERS HAD NO SADDLES; they sat bareback, clinging to the animal's mane. Next came a simple cloth saddle. The leather saddle, which was invented about 2,000 years ago by the warriors of the Asian steppes, revolutionized horseback riding. On this saddle, horsemen could gallop toward the enemy, fire arrows in all directions, and stay on their horses. Modern saddles are of two main types. The Western saddle is a heavy, working saddle used mainly by ranch hands in the United States. It has a metal horn at the front for securing a lasso and a high cantle at the back to keep the rider on the horse. The English saddle is much lighter. Designed for sport, it allows the horse to gallop fast. Its drawback is that it provides less stability; to stay on the horse, the rider must grip the animal with the knees.

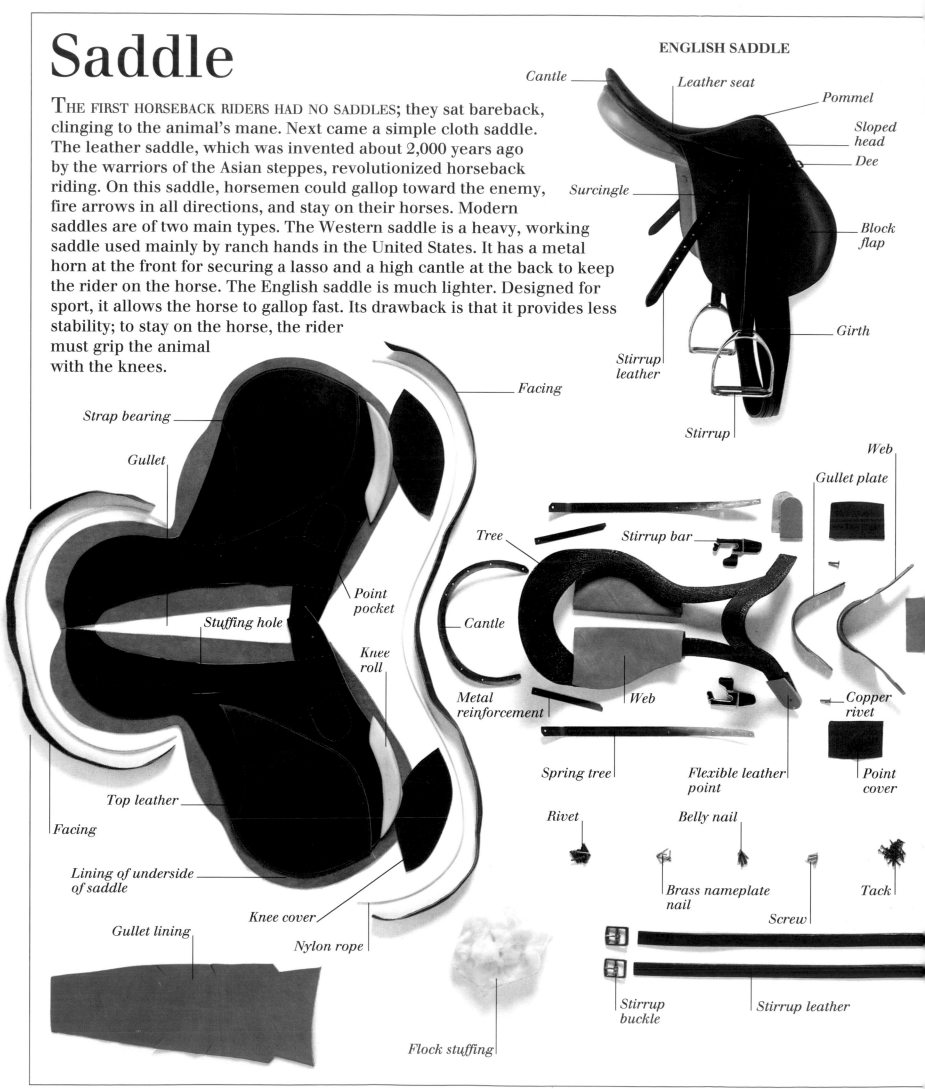

ENGLISH SADDLE

Cantle — Leather seat — Pommel — Sloped head — Dee — Surcingle — Block flap — Girth — Stirrup leather — Stirrup

Facing — Strap bearing — Gullet — Point pocket — Stuffing hole — Knee roll — Top leather — Facing — Lining of underside of saddle — Knee cover — Nylon rope — Gullet lining — Flock stuffing

Web — Gullet plate — Tree — Stirrup bar — Cantle — Metal reinforcement — Web — Copper rivet — Spring tree — Flexible leather point — Point cover — Rivet — Belly nail — Brass nameplate nail — Screw — Tack — Stirrup buckle — Stirrup leather

SHAPED GIRTH

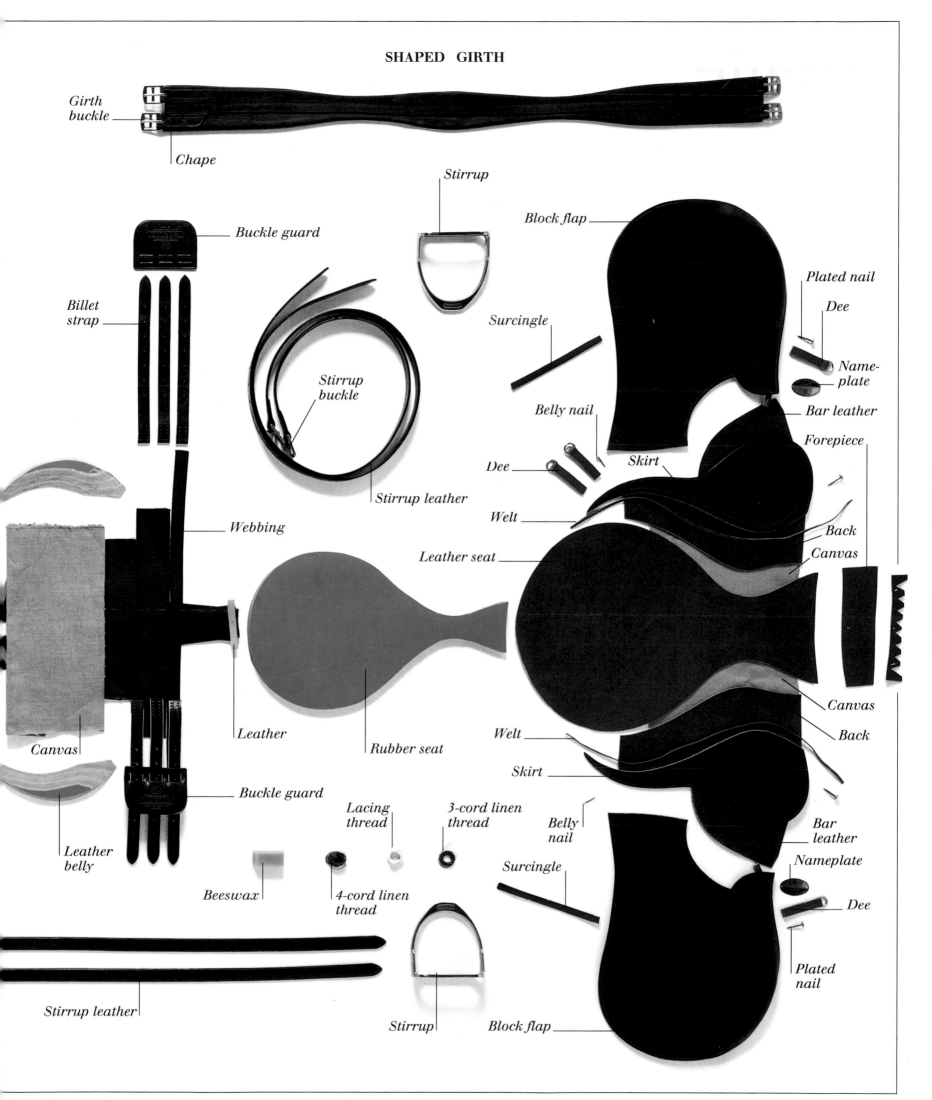

Girth buckle

Chape

Stirrup

Block flap

Buckle guard

Billet strap

Surcingle

Plated nail

Dee

Stirrup buckle

Name-plate

Belly nail

Bar leather

Dee

Skirt

Forepiece

Webbing

Welt

Back

Canvas

Stirrup leather

Leather seat

Canvas

Canvas

Leather

Welt

Back

Rubber seat

Skirt

Leather belly

Buckle guard

Belly nail

Bar leather

Lacing thread

3-cord linen thread

Nameplate

Beeswax

4-cord linen thread

Surcingle

Dee

Stirrup leather

Stirrup

Block flap

Plated nail

Espresso machine

AN ESPRESSO MACHINE MAKES the strong Italian coffee of the same name. It does this by forcing very hot water through dark-roasted, finely ground beans to extract their flavor. First, water is poured into the boiler tank until the correct level is reached (the water level can be seen in the sight glass). The machine is then switched on, and the element boils the water. When steam escapes through the steam release valve, the machine is ready to make coffee. The ground beans are measured into the filter, which rests in its holder, then the holder is slotted into the bottom of the group chamber, which channels hot water from the boiler to the coffee. A cup is placed under the spouts. The lever is then raised, opening a valve to let hot water enter the group chamber. Lowering the lever forces the hot water through the ground coffee, into the spouts, and finally into the cup. By placing a jug of milk under the steam tube and opening the steam tap, you can also heat and froth milk to make cappuccino coffee.

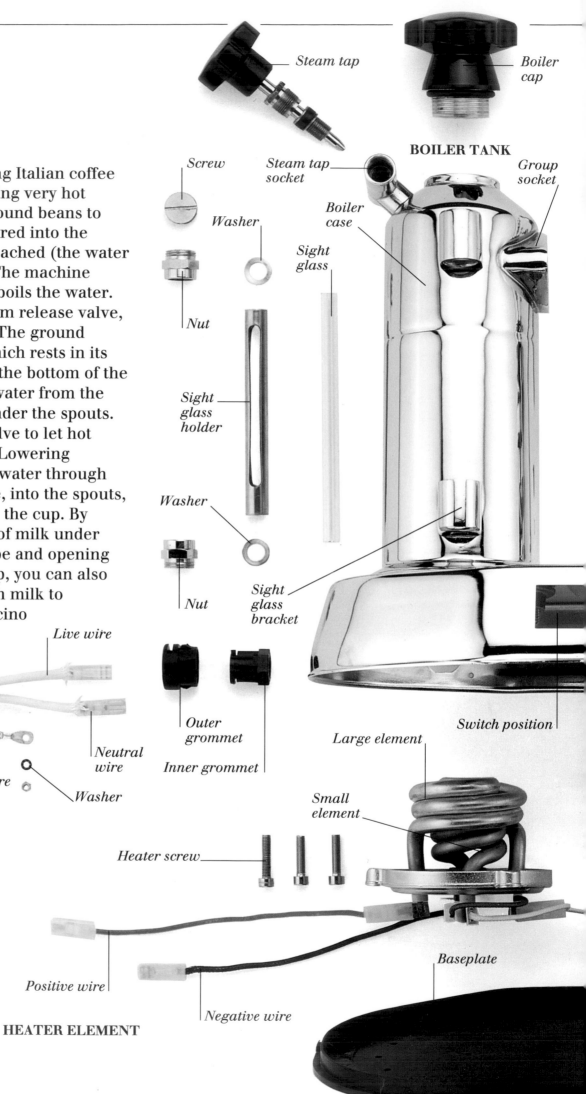

Steam tap

Boiler cap

Screw

Steam tap socket

BOILER TANK

Group socket

Washer

Boiler case

Sight glass

Nut

Sight glass holder

Washer

Nut

Sight glass bracket

Switch position

Live wire

Neutral wire

Outer grommet

Large element

Ground wire

Inner grommet

Small element

Washer

Heater screw

Lead wire

Positive wire

Negative wire

Baseplate

HEATER ELEMENT

STEAM RELEASE VALVE

Valve cap

Spring

Ball bearing

Steam release valve collar

Steam tube

Tube

Screw

Washer

Base

Maker's label

Top cap

Lock nut

GROUP

Bolt

Group tap

Group chamber

Filter plate

Group pipe

Steam jet

C-clip

Nut

Bolt

Lever

Lever handle

Coffee press

Filter

FILTER HOLDER

Handle

Spout

Measuring spoon

On/off switch

Fusible link

High/low pressure switch

Ground wire

Base screw socket

Drip grid

Drip tray

Lever handle

Lever

Group chamber

Steam tap

Steam tube

Handle

Spout

Boiler case

Sight glass tube

Sight glass bracket

Drip grid

Base

Trench coat

THE TRENCH COAT BECAME POPULAR EARLIER THIS CENTURY when half a million of them were worn by British soldiers in the First World War. Coats of this type kept combatants warm and dry in the chilly, rain-sodden trenches of northern France and Belgium. The design was so successful that, after the war, civilians also wanted to wear it. Still fashionable today, the trench coat has retained many of its original protective and military features, including the epaulettes, the storm flap on one shoulder, the belted cuffs, and the D-rings on the belt for attaching equipment. In the mid-19th century Thomas Burberry developed the waterproof, closely-woven twill fabric from which the first trench coats were made. It combined the comfort of a natural material with a strong yarn that is waterproofed before and after being tightly woven, making it comfortable and able to withstand rain.

RIGHT SLEEVE

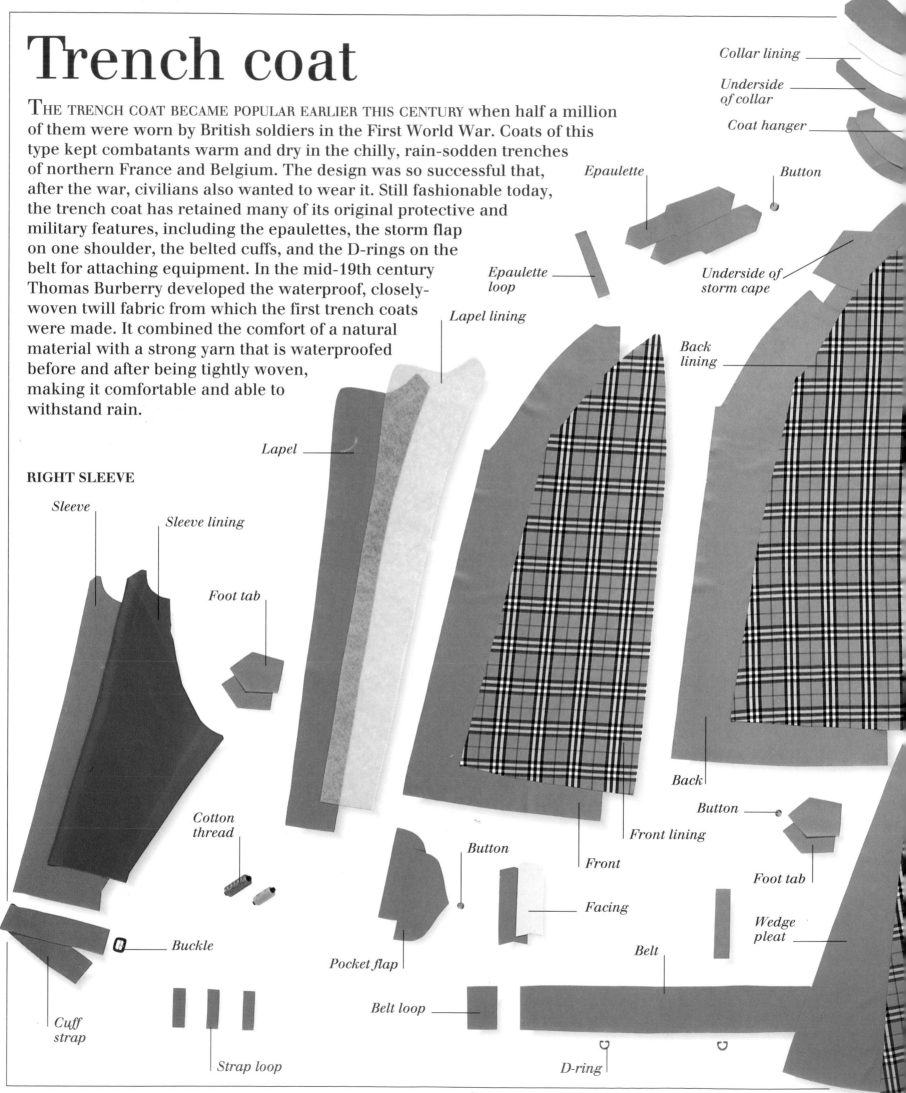

Collar lining

Underside of collar

Coat hanger

Epaulette

Button

Epaulette loop

Underside of storm cape

Lapel lining

Back lining

Lapel

Sleeve

Sleeve lining

Foot tab

Back

Button

Front lining

Foot tab

Cotton thread

Button

Front

Facing

Wedge pleat

Pocket flap

Belt

Buckle

Belt loop

Cuff strap

Strap loop

D-ring

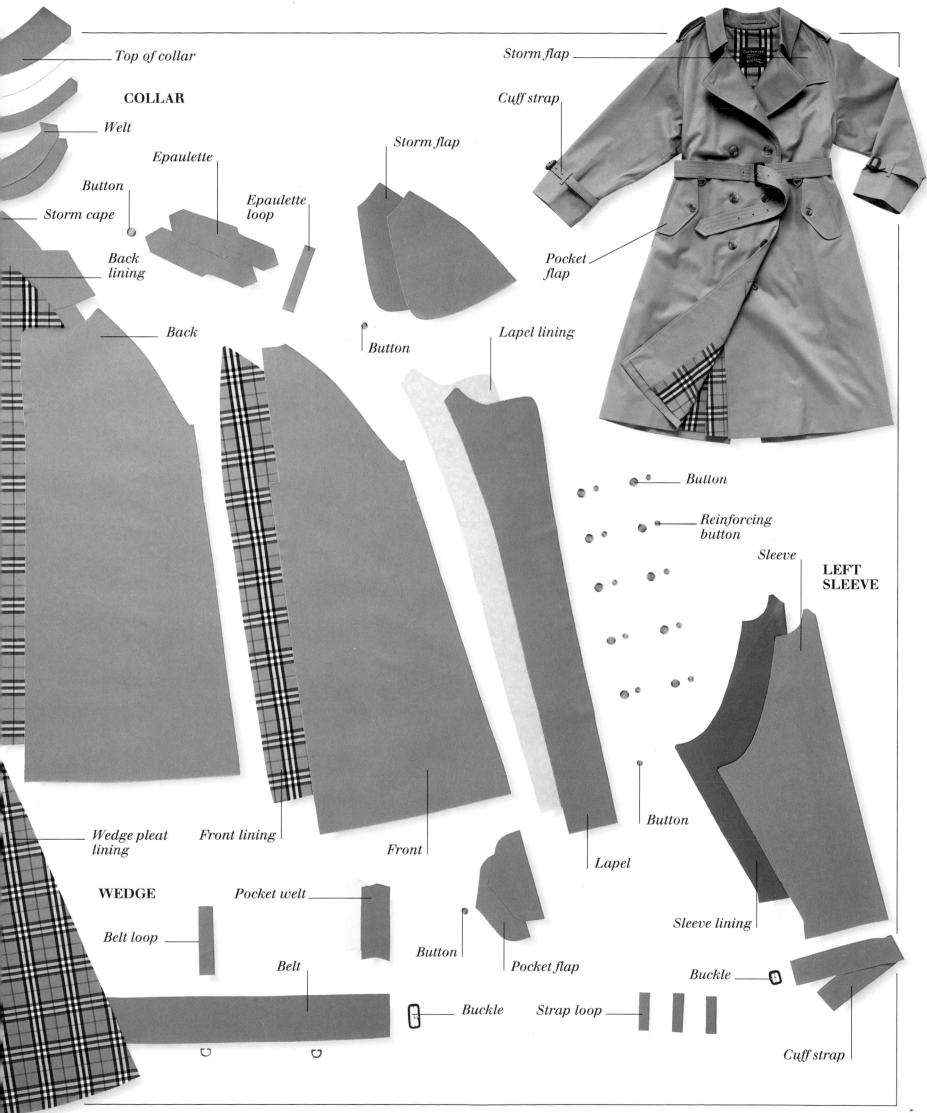

Top of collar

COLLAR

Welt

Button

Storm cape

Epaulette

Epaulette loop

Back lining

Back

Storm flap

Storm flap

Cuff strap

Pocket flap

Button

Lapel lining

Button

Reinforcing button

Sleeve

LEFT SLEEVE

Button

Wedge pleat lining

Front lining

Front

Lapel

WEDGE

Pocket welt

Belt loop

Button

Pocket flap

Sleeve lining

Belt

Buckle

Buckle

Strap loop

Buckle

Cuff strap

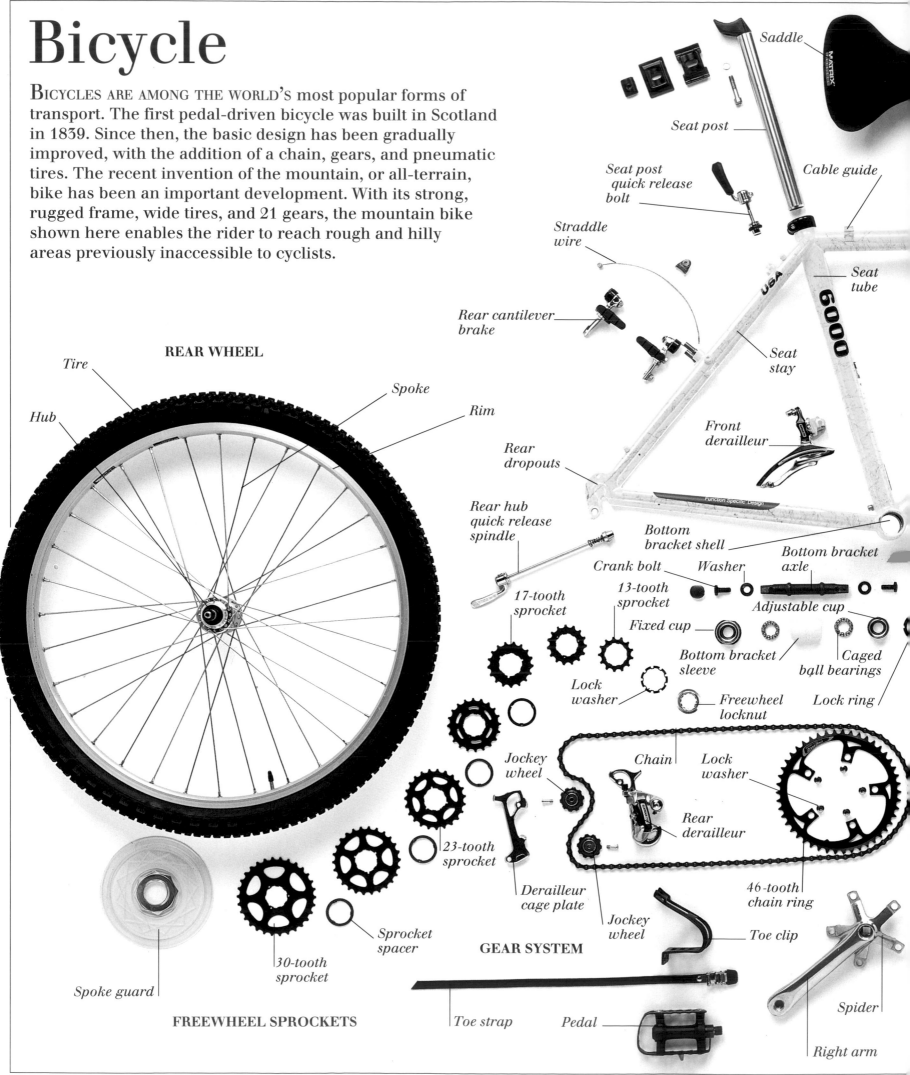

Bicycle

BICYCLES ARE AMONG THE WORLD'S most popular forms of transport. The first pedal-driven bicycle was built in Scotland in 1839. Since then, the basic design has been gradually improved, with the addition of a chain, gears, and pneumatic tires. The recent invention of the mountain, or all-terrain, bike has been an important development. With its strong, rugged frame, wide tires, and 21 gears, the mountain bike shown here enables the rider to reach rough and hilly areas previously inaccessible to cyclists.

Saddle

Seat post

Cable guide

Seat post quick release bolt

Straddle wire

Seat tube

Rear cantilever brake

Seat stay

REAR WHEEL

Tire

Spoke

Rim

Hub

Rear dropouts

Front derailleur

Rear hub quick release spindle

Bottom bracket shell

Bottom bracket axle

Crank bolt

Washer

17-tooth sprocket

13-tooth sprocket

Adjustable cup

Fixed cup

Bottom bracket sleeve

Caged ball bearings

Lock ring

Lock washer

Freewheel locknut

Chain

Lock washer

Jockey wheel

23-tooth sprocket

Rear derailleur

Derailleur cage plate

46-tooth chain ring

Jockey wheel

Sprocket spacer

Toe clip

GEAR SYSTEM

30-tooth sprocket

Spoke guard

Spider

FREEWHEEL SPROCKETS

Toe strap

Pedal

Right arm

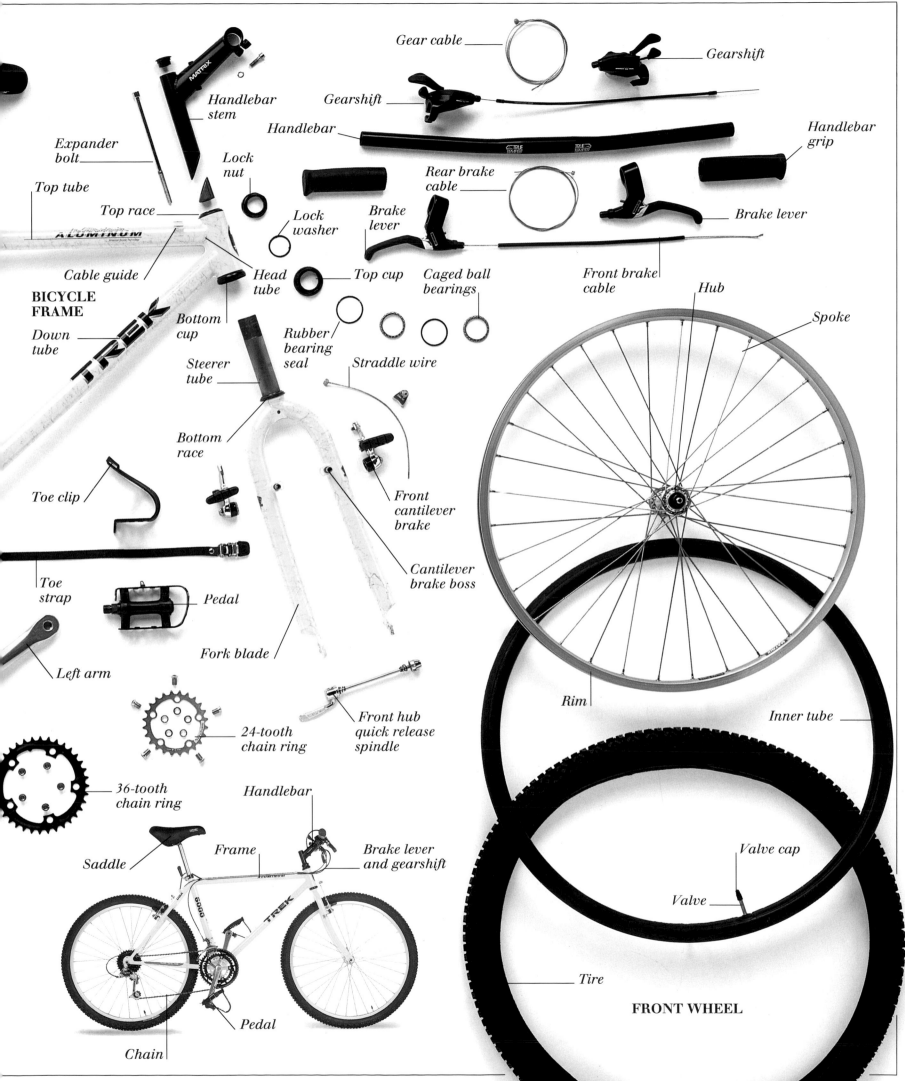

Gear cable — Gearshift

Gearshift

Handlebar

Handlebar grip

Handlebar stem

Expander bolt

Lock nut

Top tube

Top race

Lock washer

Rear brake cable

Brake lever

Brake lever

Cable guide

Head tube

Top cup

Caged ball bearings

Front brake cable

Hub

Spoke

BICYCLE FRAME

Down tube

Bottom cup

Rubber bearing seal

Steerer tube

Straddle wire

Bottom race

Toe clip

Front cantilever brake

Cantilever brake boss

Toe strap

Pedal

Fork blade

Rim

Inner tube

Left arm

24-tooth chain ring

Front hub quick release spindle

36-tooth chain ring

Handlebar

Frame

Brake lever and gearshift

Saddle

Valve cap

Valve

Pedal

Tire

FRONT WHEEL

Chain

Index

A

Aberdeen hook 18
Absorbent separator 16
Adjustable cup 58
Adjustable vane 19
Adjusting knob holder 41
Adjustment locking nut 33
Air exhaust slot 21
Air filter back 34
Air filter cover 50
Air filter front 34
Air intake slot 21
Air seal 17
Alarm reset button 14
Alkaline manganese power
  cell 16
Alkaline power cell 17
All terrain bike 58
Amplifier 14
Anatomy of a hook 18
Angle 32
Anode 16-17
Anode cap 17
Anode collector 17
Antenna 36
Antenna connector 36
Antenna holder 37
Anti-reverse device 18
Aperture 28
Aperture auto-lock
  button 29
Aperture/distance index 29
Arch 22
Arm
  Bicycle 58-59
  Chair 38
  Teddy bear 30
Armature 20
Armature spindle 20
Arm coupling 33
Arm disk 31
Arm rail 38
Arm swivel joint system 31
Artificial flies 18-19
Artificial lures 18-19
Automatic collapsible
  frame 48
Automatic collapsible
  umbrella 48
Auto-stop lever 15

B

Back
  Saddle 53
  Suit 8-9
  Trench coat 56-57
Back box 7
Back cover 28
Back cover board
  Half-bound book 27
  Leather-bound book 27
Back curtain 9
Back leg 38-39
Back lining
  Shoe 23
  Suit 8-9
  Trench coat 56-57
Back plate 7
Back rail 38
Back space key 42
Back space link 42-43
Bail arm
  Fixed-spool reel 18
  Typewriter 43
Bait 18
Ball 12-13

Ball bearing
  Espresso machine 55
  Typewriter 43
Ball bearing holder 43
Ballpoint 13
Ballpoint pen 12-13
Band
  Automatic collapsible
    umbrella 48
  Umbrella cover 48
Barb 18
Bar leather 53
Barrel
  Ballpoint pen 12-13
  Fountain pen 13
  Mechanical pencil 12
Barrel arbor hook 6
Barrel band 13
Barrel pivot hole 6
Barrel swivel 18
Barrier separator 17
Base
  Espresso machine 55
  Telephone 11
Base casing 11
Baseplate
  Espresso machine 54
  Food processor 40
  Toaster 46
  Typewriter 42
Baseplate screw 41
Base screw socket 55
Batteries 16-17
Battery
  Camera 28
  Lawnmower 50-51
Battery case lid 36
Battery chamber cap 28
Battery compartment 36
Battery connection 51
Battery contact 36
Battery cover 16
Battery level indicator 24-25
Battery retainer 51
Beam 36
Beardtrimmer 24-25
Bearing 21
Beeswax 53
Belly nail 52-53
Belt 56-57
Belt clip 14
Belted cuff 56
Belt guard 50
Belt loop
  Suit 8
  Trench coat 56-57
Bespoke suit 8
Bicycle 58-59
Bicycle frame 58-59
Billet strap 53
Bimetallic strip 46
Blade
  Cut-throat razor 24
  Food processor 40
  Lawnmower 50-51
Blade bolt 51
Blade carrier 41
Blade catch 41
Blade cover 50
Blade guard 24
Blade retainer 51
Blade insert 41
Blade screen comb 24
Block flap 52-53
Blower shroud 50
Body
  Deer hopper dry fly 19
  Lamp 32
  Suitcase 44
  Teddy bear 30

Body back 31
Body covering 28
Body disk 31
Body front 31
Body side 44
Boiler cap 54
Boiler case 54-55
Boiler tank 54
Bolt
  Espresso machine 55
  Lawnmower 50
  Toaster 46
  Typewriter 43
Bookbinding 26
Books 26-27
Bottom board 45
Bottom bracket axle 58
Bottom bracket shell 58
Bottom bracket sleeve 58
Bottom cover 28
Bottom cover assembly 28
Bottom cup 59
Bottom door 7
Bottom door key 7
Bottom filler 22-23
Bottom lining 39
Bottom race 59
Bottom splat 38
Bottom spring 49
Bottom stud 45
Bowl lock 40
Box toe 22
Brace-and-bit 20-21
Brace button 8
Bracket
  Electric shaver 24
  Lamp 32
Bracket shell 58
Brake lever 59
Brass buckle 30
Brass nameplate nail 52
Bread 46
Breast pocket 9
Bridge 7
Bridge screw 7
Broadcast transmitter 36
Brush 20
Brush holder 20
Brush spring 20
Buckle 56-57
Buckle guard 53
Buckram corner piece 26-27
Buffer spring 49
Bushing 32-33
Butt cap 19
Butt extension 19
Button
  Suit 8-9
  Trench coat 56-57
Button cell 17
Button hole silk 9
Butt section 18-19

C

Cabinet front cover 15
Cabinet rear cover 14
Cable cordset 20
Cable guide 58-59
Cable support bracket 51
Cadmium anode 17
Caged ball bearings 58-59
Cake mixer 41
Calico 38
Calico lining 38-39
Camera 28-29
Cannon pinion 7
Canopy 48-49

Cantilever brake boss 59
Cantle 52
Canvas
  Saddle 53
  Suit 8-9
Cap
  Lamp 32
  Lawnmower 50
  Mechanical pencil 12
Capacitor
  Electric shaver 25
  Mini television 37
  Telephone 11
Cap nut 32
Cappuccino coffee 54
Capstan 14
Capstan belt 15
Car battery 16
Carbon 12
Carbon brush assembly 25
Carbon contact 10
Carburetor 34
Carburetor box cover 34
Card holder 43
Card scale 43
Carriage 42-43
Carriage sub-frame 43
Carry case 14
Case
  Books 26
  Safety razor 24
Case exterior 25
Case interior 25
Case screw 25
Cassette 14
Cassette holder clamper 14
Cassette holder click arm
  assembly 14
Cassette window 14-15
Cathode 16-17
Cathode cap 17
Cathode collector 16
Cathode ray tube 36
C-clip
  Espresso machine 55
  Typewriter 42-43
Cell case 17
Cell divider 17
Cell top 17
Center element 47
Center element wire cage 47
Center hole 7
Centering magnet 36
Center wheel 6
Centrifugal brake 18
Chain
  Bicycle 58-59
  Chainsaw 34-35
Chain brake 34
Chain ring 58-59
Chainsaw 34-35
Chair 38-39
Chair frame 38
Chair rail 38
Chape 53
Charge lamp 24-25
Chassis 14
Chassis assembly 15
Check pawl 18
Check pawl cover 18
Check slide 18
Check spring 18
Cheek 19
Cheese head screw 33
Choke 37
Chopper handle 41
Chuck
  Brace-and-bit 21
  Hand drill 21
  Power drill 21

Chuck key 21
Chuck key holder 20-21
Chuck key pilot hole 21
Clamping screw 33
Clamp lower jaw 33
Clamp upper jaw 33
Clay 12
Cleaning wire 12
Clicker plate 19
Click mechanism 18
Click wheel 6
Clip
  Ballpoint pen 12-13
  Fountain pen 13
  Mechanical pencil 12
Clip screw 13
Clip screw bush 13
Clock 6-7
  Personal stereo 14
Clock case 6
Clock face 7
Clock retainer plate shield 15
Clock train 6
Cloth
  Books 26
  Suit 8
Clutch
  Fountain pen 13
  Mechanical pencil 12
  Personal stereo 15
Clutch sprocket 34-35
Coarse shredder 41
Coat hanger 56
Cock screw 7
Coffee press 55
Coil 36-37
Coil tension spring 33
Coin pocket 8
Collar
  Safety razor 24
  Suit 8-9
  Trench coat 57
Collar canvas 9
Collar lining 56
Collector
  Ballpoint pen 13
  Fountain pen 13
Collector shell 13
Collet retainer 12
Comfort control 24
Commutator 20
Cone
  Last 23
  Personal stereo 14
Connecting pin 36
Connecting wire 32
Connector
  Ballpoint pen 13
  Food processor 40
  Fountain pen 13
Control lever
  Chainsaw 34
  Lawnmower 51
Control mechanism 40
Control panel 51
Controls 40
Converter 13
Copper conductor 32
Cord
  Personal stereo 15
  Telephone 11
Cordset entry point 46
Corner piece
  Half-bound book 26
  Suitcase 44-45
Cotton thread
  Stick frame 48-49
  Trench coat 56
Counter 22-23
Counter dial cover 29

Counter dial housing 29
Counter stiffener 23
Cover
  Automatic collapsible
    umbrella 48
  Books 26
  Food processor 40
Cover board 26
Cover frame 29
Cradle switch 11
Cradle switch assembly 11
Cradle switch lever 11
Crank 21
Crank bolt 58
Creaming and egg white
  bowl 41
Creaming bowl lid 41
Cross section of a button
  cell 17
Cross section of finished
  shoe 22
Cross stick 38
CRT 36
CRT bracket 36
CRT cover 36
CRT socket 36
Crumb tray 46-47
Crutch 6
Crutch screw 6
Cuff 22
Cuff button 8-9
Cuff button facing 8-9
Cuff lining 8-9
Cuff strap 56-57
Current 16
Cutter 24
Cut-throat razor 24
Cylinder 36

D

Date button 14-15
Decorative plastic trim 10
Dee 52-53
Deer hopper dry fly 19
Deflection coil 36
Deflection yoke 36
Depth-of-field guide 29
Derailleur cage plate 58
Devon minnow 19
Dial 7
Dial foot hole 7
Dial pointer 36
Dial washer 7
Diamond 38
Diaphragm
  Camera 28
  Telephone 10
Diaphragm blade 29
Dining chair 38
Diode 11
Direct current jack 36
Disk 30-31
Disk drag 18
Disk drag housing 19
Disk spring 18
Display holder 15
Dome 32
Door 50
Door discharge 51
Door seal 50
Double-edged blade 24
Dough hook 41
Dowel 38
Dowel hole 38-39
Dowel screw 38-39
Down tube 59
Drag adjustment 18

Drag knob 19
Drag knob screw 19
Drag spindle 18
Drag washer 18
Draw cord 43
Drill bit
　Brace-and-bit 21
　Hand drill 21
　Power drill 21
Drills 20-21
D-ring 56
Drip grid 55
Drip tray 55
Drive belt
　Food processor 40
　Lawnmower 50
Drive cog 34
Drive handle 51
Drive shaft
　Electric shaver 24
　Food processor 40
　Lawnmower 50
Drive shaft gear 40
Drive wheel
　Food processor 40
　Hand drill 21
Dual click gear 18
Dunkeld wet fly 19
Dustcover for earpiece 10
Dustcover for mouthpiece 10

E

Ear 30
Ear back 30
Ear front 30
Earphone 14-15
Earphone jack 36
Earpiece 10
Earpiece transducer 10
East-West amplifier
　integrated circuit 36
E-clip 34
Ejector assembly 47
Ejector bracket 46-47
Ejector lever 47
Electrical circuit 46
Electrically driven motor 34
Electrical signal 10
Electric current 14
Electric motor 40
Electric shaver 24
Electric toaster 46
Electrolyte 16
Electrolytic capacitor 36
Electromagnet
　Telephone 10
　Toaster 46
Electromagnetic induction
　capacitor 20
Electron beam 36
Electron flow 16
Electron gun 36
Electronic signal 42
Element retaining stop 47
End baffle plate 46-47
End cap 32-33
End element 46-47
End element connecting link
　46-47
End element wire
　guard 46-47
Endpaper
　Half-bound book 26-27
　Leather-bound book 27
Engine 50
Engine and recoil
　assembly 50

Engine pulley 50
English saddle 52
Epaulette 56-57
Epaulette loop 56-57
Eraser 12
Escapement body 43
Escapement dog 43
Escape wheel 6
Espresso machine 54-55
Exchange number 11
Expander bolt 59
Exposure 28
Exposure counter 28-29
Exposure counter dial 29
Extra-high tension lead 37
Eye
　Anatomy of a hook 18
　Deer hopper dry fly 19
　Devon minnow 19
　Nib 13
　Teddy bear 30
Eyelet 22-23

F

Fabric 48
Facing
　Saddle 52
　Suit 9
　Trenchcoat 56
Facing of lapel 8-9
Fan 20
Fan housing 34
Fan vent 35
Fanwheel 34
Fastening 8
Fast-forward and rewind
　pulley assembly 15
Fast-forward button 14
Fast-forward gear 15
Feed 13
Feed roll 43
Feed tube 40
Felt 30
Female lead connector 14
Ferrule 49
Field 20
Filament 32
Filler unit
　Ballpoint pen 13
　Fountain pen 13
Filling funnel 40
Film 28
Film chamber 28
Film guide rail 28
Film pressure plate 28
Film rail 28
Film rewind/back cover
　release knob 28-29
Film rewind crank 28-29
Film roller 28
Film speed indicator 29
Film sprocket spool 28
Film take-up spool 28
Film wind lever 29
Filter
　Espresso machine 55
　Mini television 37
Filter holder 55
Filter ornament 37
Filter plate 55
Fin 19
Fine shredder 41
Fire safety 38
Fishing tackle 18-19
Fixed cup 58
Fixed-spool reel 18
Fixing screw 47

Flashgun 28
Flexible leather point 52
Flock stuffing 52
Fly back transformer 37
Fly button 9
Fly cap
　Automatic collapsible
　　frame 48-49
　Stick frame 48-49
Flyleaf 27
Fly reel 18-19
Fly rod 18-19
Flywheel
　Chainsaw 34
　Lawnmower 50
Foam padding 38-39
Focus control 37
Focusing ring 29
Food processor 40-41
Foot
　Food processor 41
　Toaster 46-47
Footpad 31
Footpad reinforcement 31
Foot tab 56
Fore edge
　Half-bound book 26
　Leather-bound book 27
Forepart 8-9
Forepart lining 8-9
Forepiece 53
Fork blade 59
Fountain pen 12-13
Frame 59
Freewheel locknut 58
Freewheel sprocket 58
French bearer 9
French fries cutter 41
Front 56-57
Front board assembly 28
Front brake cable 59
Front cabinet 37
Front cantilever brake 59
Front cover board
　Half-bound book 26
　Leather-bound book 27
Front derailleur 58
Front hackle 19
Front handle 35
Front hub quick release
　spindle 59
Frontispiece 27
Front leg
　Chair 38-39
　Suit 8
Front lens frame retainer
　plate 28
Front lens group 28
Front lining 56-57
Front plate 6
Front rail 38
Front tire 50
Front wheel
　Bicycle 59
　Lawnmower 50-51
Fuel filler cap 34
Fuel tank 50
Fuel tank cap 51
Function button seal 14
Fusee 6
Fusee chain 6
Fuse enclosure 32
Fusee pivot hole 6
Fusee stop 6
Fusee stop screw 6
Fusible link 55

G

Gallop 52
Gape 18
Garment 8
Gasoline-driven motor 34
Gear 40
Gear cable 59
Gearcase 21
Gearcase assembly 50
Gearcase cover 21
Gearcase cover screw 21
Gearcase position 20
Gearcase screw 21
Gear cover 24
Gear frame 24
Gearing system 18
Gear mechanism 21
Gear retainer 18
Gears
　Clock 6
　Drills 20
　Lawnmower 50
Gearshift 59
Gear system
　Bicycle 58
　Electric shaver 24
Gear wheel 24
Gimp 9
Girth 52
Girth buckle 53
Glass envelope 32
Glue
　Books 26
　Chair 38
　Mini television 37
Gold tooling 26-27
Golfball 42
Gore 48-49
Graphite 12
Graphite pencil 12
Grass bag 51
Grass bag frame 51
Grater 41
Groove 38
Ground coffee 54
Ground connection
　point 46
Ground speed control
　knob 51
Ground wire 54-55
Group 55
Group chamber 54-55
Group pipe 55
Group socket 54
Group tap 55
Guide 8
Guide bar 34-35
Guide bar nut 35
Gullet 52
Gullet lining 52
Gullet plate 52

H

Hackle 19
Half-bound book 26
Half pulley 50
Hammer actuator
　position 20
Hammer mechanism 20
Hammer mechanism
　actuator 20-21
Hand-bound book 26
Hand collet 7
Hand drill 20-21
Handgrip 18
Hand guard 34-35

Handle
　Automatic collapsible
　　frame 48-49
　Automatic collapsible
　　umbrella 48
　Brace-and-bit 21
　Cut-throat razor 24
　Espresso machine 55
　Fixed-spool reel 18
　Fly reel 19
　Food processor 40-41
　Lawnmower 51
　Multiplier reel 18
　Safety razor 24
　Stick frame 48-49
　Stick umbrella 49
　Suitcase 44
　Umbrella 48-49
Handle and traction control
　assembly 51
Handlebar 59
Handlebar grip 59
Handlebar stem 59
Handle trim 44
Handset 11
Handset back cover 11
Handset cord 11
Handset cord plug 11
Handset front cover 10
Hardback book 26
Hardware buckle 45
Hardware buckle catch 44
Head
　Brace-and-bit 21
　Chair 38-39
　Deer hopper dry fly 19
　Dunkeld wet fly 19
　Teddy bear 30
Headband
　Half-bound book 26
　Leather-bound book 27
Headphone jack 14
Headphone socket
　packing 14
Headset 15
Head tube 59
Hearing aid 16
Heater element 54
Heater screw 54
Heel
　Nib 13
　Shoes 22-23
Heel grip 22
Heel nail 23
Height adjuster 50
Hexagon nut
　Chainsaw 34
　Lamp 33
High/low pressure switch 55
Hillman anti-kink weight 18
Hinge 23
Hinged brass bezel 7
Hip flap pocket 9
Hole
　Camera 29
　Telephone 11
Hook 18-19
Horizontal frequency
　adjustment 37
Hot shoe 29
Hour hand 7
Hour hand screw 7
Hour marker 7
Hour wheel 7
Housing
　Food processor 40
　Lawnmower 50-51
Housing cover 20-21
Housing cover screw 21
Hub 58-59

I

Ignition module 34
Ink 12
Ink tube 13
Inlet 25
Inner cage assembly 47
Inner cap 13
Inner grommet 54
Inner sock 22-23
Inner tube 59
Inside cap 49
Inside cap wire 49
Inside pocket 8
Inside quarter 22
Insole 22
Insole with ribbing 23
Installing ring 29
Installing ring retainer
　plate 28
Insulating seal ring 17
Insulation 32
Integrated circuit 11
Interior sheeting 45
Interior strap 45
Interior zipper pocket 45
Intermediate frequency
　coil 37
Intermediate ring 19
Internal battery cover 15
Iridium tip 13

J

Jacket 8
Jacket button 8
Jacket hanger 8
Jack-locating hole 23
Jaw
　Brace-and-bit 21
　Hand drill 21
　Power drill 21
Jockey wheel 58
Joint
　Chair 38
　Jointed plug 19
　Leather-bound book 26-27
Jointed plug 19
Jointer 14

K

Keeper ring 18
Key
　Suitcase 44
　Typewriter 42
Key pad casing 10
Key pad contact 11
Key pad membrane 10
Keystone amplifier
　integrated circuit 36
Key top
　Telephone 10
　Typewriter 42-43
Knee cover 52
Knee roll 52

L

Lacing thread 53
Lamp 32-33
Lamp holder 32
Lamp holder coupling 33
Lapel 56-57

Lapel lining 56-57
Lap hair 8-9
Large element 54
Lasso 52
Last 22-23
Latch handle 51
Lawnmower **50-51**
Lead
  Fishing tackle 18
  Mechanical pencil 12
Lead acid car battery 16
Lead guard 12
Lead metal negative plate 16
Lead oxide positive plate 16
Lead pencil 12
Lead tube 12
Lead wire
  Espresso machine 54
  Power drill 20
Leather
  Books 26
  Saddle 52-53
  Shoes 22
Leather belly 53
Leather-bound book 26-27
Leather collar 30
Leather cover 26-27
Leather saddle 52
Leather seat 52-53
Leg
  Chair 38-39
  Suit 8-9
  Teddy bear 30-31
Leg disk 31
Leg swivel joint system 31
Lens 28
Lens alignment node 29
Lens barrel assembly 28
Lens lock release lever 28-29
Lens mount 28
Lenticular bob 6
Letter 42
Level-wind system 18
Lever 54-55
Lever handle 55
Lid 40
Light 28
Light bulb 32
Line 18-19
Line guide 19
Line guide cover 19
Linen thread 53
Line spacing lever 42
Line spacing linkage 42
Lining
  Half-bound book 26
  Leather-bound book 27
  Saddle 52
  Shoes 22
  Suit 8-9
Link 49
Liquid crystal display
  clock 15
Lithium manganese power
  cell 17
Live wire 54
Lock button 20
Locking nut 33
Lock nut
  Bicycle 59
  Chainsaw 34
  Espresso machine 55
Lock ring 58
Lock spring 48
Lock washer 58-59
Logo 44
Logo patch 44
Lure 18

M

Made-to-measure suit 8
Magnet
  Mini television 36
  Toaster 46
Magnetic field 14
Magnetic pattern 14
Magnetic tape 14
Main barrel assembly 29
Main body 29
Mainframe assembly 42
Main handle 21
Main integrated circuit 14
Main mounted printed
  circuit board 14
Main rib 48
Mains lead 24
Mainspring
  Automatic collapsible
    frame 48-49
  Clock 6
Mainspring barrel 6
Mainspring barrel arbor 6
Mainspring barrel cap 6
Mainspring drum 43
Maker's label 55
Maker's name 7
Manganese dioxide and
  graphite cathode 16
Manila 26
Marbleized paper 26-27
Margin rack 43
Margin stop 43
Material 9
Measuring cup 41
Measuring scale 40
Measuring spoon 55
Mechanical brake 18
Mechanical pencil 12
Memory button 10
Mercury power cell 17
Metal arm 33
Metal case 12
Metal chain 34
Metal collet 12
Metal fitting 44
Metal frame 45
Metal horn 52
Metal reinforcement 52
Metal shade 32-33
Metal shield 34
Metal slider 44
Microphone 10-11
Mini television **36-37**
Minute hand 7
Minute track 7
Minute wheel 7
Minute wheel cock 7
Mode button 15
Mohair 30
Mortice 38-39
Mortice slot 38
Motor
  Electric shaver 25
  Food processor 40
  Power drill 20
Motor assembly
  Personal stereo 15
  Power drill 20
Motor block 40
Motor bracket 15
Motor case
  Electric shaver 25
  Power drill 20
Motor control integrated
  circuit 14
Motor lead 25
Motor position 20
Motor speed preset 14

Mountain bike 58
Mounting bracket 36
Mouth 30
Mouthpiece 10
Moving picture 36
Mower drive handle 51
Muffler
  Chainsaw 35
  Lawnmower 50
Muffler cover 50-51
Mull
  Half-bound book 26
  Leather-bound book 27
Multiplier reel 18

N

Nail
  Automatic collapsible
    frame 48-49
  Shoes 22
Nameplate 53
Nameplate ring 28
Name tag 44
Neck disk 31
Needle cage 35
Negative battery contact 15
Negative electrode 16
Negative pole 36
Negative terminal
  Lead acid car battery 16
  Rechargeable nickel-
    cadmium power cell 17
Negative wire 54
Neutral wire 54
Nib 12-13
Nickel-cadmium power cell
  16-17
Nickel oxide cathode 17
Nickel plated steel case 17
Nipple 36
Nose
  Mechanical pencil 12
  Teddy bear 30
Notch 49
Notched lapel 9
Notch wire 49
Number list 10
Nut
  Espresso machine 54-55
  Lamp 33
  Toaster 46
  Typewriter 42-43
Nylon rope 52
Nylon seal 17

O

Oil dipstick 50
Oil filler cap 34
Oil fill tube 50
On/off indicator 25
On/off knob 25
On/off switch
  Electric shaver 24
  Espresso machine 55
  Food processor 40
On/off switch backplate 25
On/off switch frontplate 25
Open cap 49
Opening and closing
  plate 29
Operating link 43
Ornamental strip 37
Ornament ring 28
Outer cap 12-13

Outer case 25
Outer grommet 54
Outer steel jacket 16-17
Outside quarter 22-23
Outsole 22-23
Over cap 12-13

P

Padding 8-9
Padlock 44
Page 26
Pallet 6
Pallet arbor 6
Pallet arbor position 6
Pallet cock 6
Pallet cock screw 6
Pallet screw 6
Panel assembly 25
Pants 8-9
Paper 26
Paper pan 43
Paper release lever 43
Parasol 48
Pastedown
  Half-bound book 26-27
  Leather-bound book 27
Pattern 8
Paw 30
Pawpad 31
Pawpad reinforcement 31
Pedal 58-59
Pedal driven bicycle 58
Pencils 12-13
Pendulum 6
Pendulum assembly 6
Pendulum rod 6
Pens **12-13**
Pentaprism 29
Perforated wing cap 22
Personal stereo **14-15**
Personal stereo clock 14
Phosphor 36
Photographic film 28
Piercer tube 13
Piercing 13
Piezo tone ringer 11
Pillar 6
Pillar hole 7
Pin 7
Pinch roller 14-15
Pinion
  Clock 6
  Hand drill 21
Pivot
  Cut-throat razor 24
  Lamp 33
Pivot hole 6
Pivot plate 32-33
Plain end casing 47
Plastic cap 37
Plastic grommet 17
Plastic mold 22
Plastic sheath 37
Plated nail 53
Platen 42-43
Platen knob 43
Plate-nut 18
Plate separator 16
Playback head 14-15
Play button 14
Plug
  Electric shaver 25
  Mechanical pencil 12
Plug socket 24-25
Plunger contact 32
Pneumatic tire 58
Pocket facing 8-9

Pocket flap
  Suit 8-9
  Trench coat 56-57
Pocket jet 9
Pocket jet facing 8-9
Pocket lining 8
Pocket welt
  Suit 9
  Trench coat 57
Point 18
Point cover 52
Point pocket 52
Polyester stuffing 31
Pommel 52
Portable cassette player 14
Positive electrode 16
Positive pole 36
Positive terminal
  Lead acid car battery 16
  Rechargeable nickel-
    cadmium power cell 17
Positive wire 54
Power cell 16
Power dial 37
Power drill **20-21**
Power indicator 14
Power supply cord
  Lamp 32-33
  Toaster 46
Power switch 37
Precision screw 15
Press 26
Press stud 48
Pressure 12
Printed circuit board
  Electric shaver 25
  Mini television 37
  Personal stereo 14-15
  Telephone 10-11
Prism retainer plate 29
Prism retainer spring 29
Protective battery
  contact 14
Protective cap 24
Punchhole 22
Push button key pad 10
Pusher 41
Push switch 32

Q

Quarter and counter
  lining 23
Quarter backer 22-23
Quarter lining 22
Quarter tip 23
Quick release spindle 58-59
Quill 21

R

Ratchet
  Brace-and-bit 21
  Fixed-spool reel 18
Ratchet pawl 6
Ratchet screw 6
Rating nut 6
Razors **24-25**
Ready-made suit 8
Rear brake cable 59
Rear cabinet 36
Rear cantilever brake 58
Rear derailleur 58
Rear drop outs 58
Rear handle 35
Rear handle molding 34

Rear hub quick release
  spindle 58
Rear lens group 29
Rear tire 50
Rear wheel
  Bicycle 58
  Lawnmower 50-51
Receiver 10
Rechargeable battery 16
Rechargeable battery cell 25
Recoil case 50-51
Recoil rope rotor 34
Rectifier 25
Redial button 10
Reel
  Fishing tackle 18-19
  Personal stereo 14
Reel foot
  Fixed-spool reel 18
  Fly reel 18-19
  Multiplier reel 18
Reel printed circuit board
  riveting 15
Reel scoop
  Fixed-spool reel 18
  Fly reel 18-19
  Multiplier reel 18
Reel seat 19
Regency-style carver 38
Reinforcement 15
Reinforcing button 57
Release button
  Automatic collapsible
    frame 48-49
  Automatic collapsible
    umbrella 48
Release catch 24
Release lever 19
Release spring 19
Resealable vent
  mechanism 17
Reservoir 12
Resistor 11
Retainer 34-35
Retainer screw 28-29
Retaining plate assembly 24
Retaining screw
  Fly reel 18-19
  Telephone 11
Retractable pull-handle 44
Return spring 11
Reversed bend hook 18
Reverse of marbleized
  paper 27
Rewind belt 15
Rewind button 14
Rewind shaft 29
Rewind shaft bushing 29
Rib
  Automatic collapsible
    frame 48-49
  Leather-bound book 26-27
  Stick frame 48-49
  Stick umbrella 49
Ribbing
  Dunkeld wet fly 19
  Shoes 22
Ribbon
  Leather-bound book 26-27
  Typewriter 42-43
Ribbon cable 11
Ribbon carrier 43
Ribbon drive 43
Ribbon drive link 43
Ribbon drive pawl 43
Ribbon mechanism 43
Ribbon shaft 43
Ribbon spool 42-43
Rib tip 48
Right-angle jack 14

Rim 58-59
Ringer on/off switch 11
Ring seal 14
Rivet
    Saddle 52
    Shoes 22
    Stick frame 48-49
Rod 18
Roman numeral 7
Rope 34-35
Rope rotor 34
Rotating blade 24
Rotating tray 40
Rotor 25
Rubber 22
Rubber bearing seal 59
Rubber foot back 11
Rubber sealing washer 10
Rubber seat 53
Runner
    Automatic collapsible
        frame 48-49
    Stick frame 48-49
Runner cover 48
Runner wire 48

S

Saddle 52-53
    Bicycle 58-59
Saddle lining 52
Safety 40
Safety fuse display 40
Safety fuse resistor 25
Safety interlock 40-41
Safety interlock lever 40
Safety razor 24
Safety washer 30-31
Scan coil clamp 36
Scan coil deflection yoke 36
Screen 36
Screen panel 51
Screw
    Automatic collapsible
        frame 48-49
    Chainsaw 34-35
    Chair 38-39
    Espresso machine 54-55
    Fly reel 18-19
    Food processor 40
    Lawnmower 50-51
    Mini television 36
    Personal stereo 15
    Power drill 20
    Saddle 52
    Suitcase 44-45
    Teddy bear 30-31
    Telephone 10-11
    Toaster 46
    Typewriter 43
Screw hole
    Clock 7
    Electric shaver 25
    Power drill 20
Screw locking nut 19
Screw plug 40
Seat cover 39
Seat frame 39
Seat lift 22-23
Seatpad 38
Seat post 58
Seat post quick release
    bolt 58
Seat rail 39
Seat rivet 23
Seat stay 58
Seat tube 58
Seat upholstery 39

Section
    Half-bound book 26
    Leather-bound book 27
Security clasp 45
Segment 42
Segment slot 42
Selector switch 46-47
Self tap screw 34
Separator 17
Serrated blade 24
Shade coupling 33
Shaft 20
Shank
    Anatomy of a hook 18
    Shoes 22-23
Shaped girth 53
Shaver case exterior 25
Shavers 24-25
Shaving head 24
Shaving head holder 24
Shelter 48
Shift key 42
Shift link 43
Shift lock key 42
Shoelace 22-23
Shoe pocket 45
Shoes 22-23
Shoulder pad 8-9
Shoulder screw 55
Shredder 41
Shroud 34
Shutter 28
Shutter cocked indicator 29
Shutter curtain 28
Shutter dial knob spring 29
Shutter release button 28-29
Shutter speed dial 28-29
Shutter speed index 29
Side handle 21
Side inspection door 7
Side of head 30
Side plate 18
Side pocket 8-9
Side rail 38
Side strip panel 25
Sight glass 54
Sight glass bracket 54-55
Sight glass holder 54
Sight glass tube 55
Signal
    Mini television 36
    Telephone 10
Signature
    Half-bound book 26
    Leather-bound book 27
Silver oxide button cell 16
Sinker 18
Skirt
    Lamp 32
    Saddle 53
Sleeve
    Batteries 17
    Suit 8-9
    Trench coat 56-57
Sleeve head wadding 8-9
Sleeve lining 56-57
Slicer 41
Slicer knob 41
Slit 13
Sloped head 52
Small element 54
Socket
    Lamp 33
    Telephone 11
Solar power pack 15
Solder joint 11
Sole 22
Sound waves
    Personal stereo 14
    Telephone 10

Space bar 42
Spark plug 34
Spatula 41
Speaker 37
Speed dial knob 29
Speed selector 40
Speed settings 40
Sphere 42
Spider 58
Spigot 33
Spiked bumper 35
Spindle gear 21
Spine
    Half-bound book 26
    Leather-bound book 26-27
Spine edge 26
Spine piece 26
Splat 38
Splat mortice 38-39
Spoke 58-59
Spoke guard 58
Spool 18
Spool cover 19
Spool-release button
    Fly reel 19
    Multiplier reel 18
Spool screw 19
Sport 52
Spout 54-55
Spreader wire 48
Spring
    Ballpoint 13
    Ballpoint pen 13
    Electric shaver 24-25
    Espresso machine 55
    Lawnmower 50
    Mechanical pencil 12
    Personal stereo 14-15
    Power drill 20
    Toaster 47
    Typewriter 42-43
    Umbrella 48-49
Spring attachment 33
Spring attachment bolt 33
Spring tree 52
Sprocket 58
Sprocket cover 35
Sprocket spacer 58
Spur gear 40
Square brass line 38
Stainless steel cover 47
Star wheel 43
Star drag 18
Starter cup 50
Starter grip 34-35
Starter rope 34
Stay tape 8-9
Steady pin hole 6
Steam jet 55
Steam release valve 55
Steam release valve
    collar 55
Steam tap 54-55
Steam tap socket 54
Steam tube 54-55
Steel jacket 16
Steerer tube 59
Stereo jack plug 14
Stereo sound 14
Stick frame 49
Stick umbrella 48-49
Stirrup 52-53
Stirrup bar 52
Stirrup buckle 52-53
Stirrup leather 52-53
Stitching 48
Stop button 14
Stopping pin 49
Storm cape 57
Storm flap 56-57

Straddle wire 58-59
Strain release 46
Strap bearing 52
Strap loop 56-57
Strap lug 28-29
Stretcher
    Automatic collapsible
        frame 48-49
    Stick frame 48-49
Stuffing hole 52
Sub-frame 42
Subject distance scale 29
Suit 8-9
Suitcase 44-45
Suitcase body 44
Suitcase interior 45
Supply reel 15
Support arm assembly 33
Supporter ring 29
Supporter ring retainer
    plate 29
Support ring 17
Support wire 32
Surcingle 52-53
Suspension spring 6
Switch 20
Switch enclosure 32
Switch enclosure cover 32
Switch end casting 46-47
Switch position
    Electric shaver 25
    Espresso machine 54
Switch trigger 20-21
Swivel 18-19
Symbol 42

T

Table clamp 33
Table clamp assembly 33
Tack
    Chair 39
    Saddle 52
Tag 23
Tail
    Deer hopper dry fly 19
    Dunkeld wet fly 19
    Half-bound book 26
    Leather-bound book 26
Tailband
    Half-bound book 26
    Leather-bound book 27
Tailor 8
Tailor tack 8
Take-up reel 15
Tank housing 34
Tape
    Half-bound book 26
    Leather-bound book 27
    Mini television 36
    Personal stereo 14
    Suit 9
Tape end sensor 15
Tape select 14
Tape select lever 15
Tape speed adjustment
    packing 14
Tape type selector 14
Tapping screw 15
Tassie 12-13
Tassie screw 13
Teddy bear 30-31
Teeth 34
Telephone 10-11
Telephone cord 11
Telephone cord plug 11
Telephone handset 10
Television set 36

Tenon 38-39
Tenon tongue 38
Tension gear plate
    riveting 15
Tension nut 18
Tension roller gear 15
Tension spring 6
Tension spring screw 6
Terminal connection 46
Terminal screw 32
Thimble 23
Third wheel 6
Thread
    Leather-bound book 27
    Shoes 23
    Teddy bear 31
Threaded rod 33
Three-piece suit 8
Throat 18
Throttle control lever 51
Throttle guard 50
Throttle rod 34
Thrust plate 21
Thrust washer 21
Time switch 46
Tine 13
Tip
    Automatic collapsible
        frame 48-49
    Automatic collapsible
        umbrella 48
    Stick frame 48-49
    Stick umbrella 49
Tip cup
    Stick frame 48-49
    Stick umbrella 49
Tip ring 19
Tip section 19
Toaster 46-47
Toe clip 58-59
Toe strap 58-59
Tongue 22
Tongue lining 22
Tooth 35
Top cap 55
Top casing 10
Top collar 8
Top corner piece 44
Top cover 29
Top cover assembly 29
Top cup 55
Top insert blank 20
Top leather 52
Top of body 31
Top of collar 57
Top plate 42
Top race 59
Top sleeve 8-9
Top splat 38
Top spring
    Automatic collapsible
        frame 48-49
    Stick frame 48-49
Top tube 59
Torsion spring 40
Traction cable 51
Traction cable support 51
Traction lever 51
Transformer 25
Transistor 11
Transport 58
Tray 41
Treble hook
    Devon minnow 19
    Fishing tackle 18
    Jointed plug 19
Tree 52
Trench coat 56-57
Trigger mechanism 20
Trigger position 20

Trim 45
Trimmer blade 25
Trimmer operating lever 24
Trimmer release 25
Trimming 26
Trim patch 44-45
Tripod socket hole 28
Trouser clasp 9
Tube
    Espresso machine 55
    Stick frame 48-49
    Stick umbrella 49
Tube neck 36
Tulip mount 19
Tuner 36
Tuning dial 36
Tuning drive gear 36
Tuning printed circuit
    board 36
Turning handle 21
Two-core shielded wire 15
Two-piece suit 8-9
Type 42
Type bar 42-43
Type bar link 42-43
Type guide 42
Type key lever 43
Typewriter 42-43
Typewriter case 42
Tire 58-59

U

Umbrellas 48-49
Undercollar 9
Underside of collar 56
Underside of storm cape 56
Under sleeve 8-9
Unskirted spool 18
Upper gear case 50
Uppers 22

V

Valve 59
Valve cap
    Bicycle 59
    Espresso machine 55
Vamp 22
Vamp backer 23
Variable time control knob
    46-47
Vent
    Alkaline manganese
        power cell 17
    Suit 8
Vent plug 16
Vertical panel 51
Vest 8
Viewfinder eyepiece 28-29
Viewing system 28
Voice box 31
Volume control 14
Volume control dial 37

W

Waistband 9
Washer 21
    Alkaline manganese
        power cell 16-17
    Automatic collapsible
        frame 48-49
    Bicycle 58

Washer (continued)
  Camera 28-29
  Chainsaw 34
  Chair 38
  Electric shaver 24
  Espresso machine 54-55
  Food processor 40
  Lamp 33
  Lawnmower 51
  Personal stereo 15
  Power drill 20-21
  Stick frame 48-49
  Suitcase 44-45
  Teddy bear 30-31
  Telephone 11
  Toaster 46-47

Typewriter 43
Web 52
Webbing
  Chair 38-39
  Saddle 53
  Suitcase 44
Wedge 57
Wedge pleat 56
Wedge pleat lining 57
Weight 18
Welt
  Saddle 53
  Shoes 22-23
  Trench coat 57
Western saddle 52
Wheel 45

Wheel bolt 50-51
Wheel cover
  Lawnmower 50
  Suitcase 45
Whisk 41
Whisk driving arm 41
Wide feed tube 41
Winding hole 7
Winding key 6
Wind lever collar 29
Wind lever install
  spring 29
Window
  Camera 29
  Mini television 37
  Telephone 10

Wing
  Deer hopper dry fly 19
  Nib 13
Wing cap 22
Wing cap and vamp lining 22
Wing cap backer 22
Wing nut 32-33
Wire
  Personal stereo 14
  Telephone 11
Wire frame 44-45
Wire spring 25
Wood 12
Wood bezel 7
Wood frame 38
Wood mold 22

Wood peg 6-7
Wood plug 38
Wood stick 12
Wood wool 30
Wood wool stuffing 30-31
Working bowl 40
Working saddle 52
Worklamp 32

X

X-contact 29
X-flash sync cap 28
X-flash sync terminal 28

Y

Yarn 56
Yoke 36

Z

Zinc air button cell 17
Zinc gel anode 17
Zipper 45

Acknowledgments

Dorling Kindersley would like to thank:
Active Clock Repair; City Clocks (Clocks); Agnews Tailors; Hacket; Paul Stewart (Suit); Audioline Ltd; S A Jackson; Precision Interconnect (Telephone); Arthur Brown & Co. Inc.; Berol Ltd; Parker Pen Co; Penfriend (London) Ltd; Philip Poole & Co Ltd; Rotring UK Ltd (Pencils and pens); Christopher Cullen, Babber Electronics; Golan Harris; Sony UK Ltd (Personal stereo; Mini television); Duracell International Inc.; Exide Batteries Ltd (Batteries); Capitol Fishing Tackle; Farlows of Pall Mall; House of Hardy; Leeda Fishing Tackle (Fishing tackle); Black and Decker Inc. (Drills); British Footwear Manufacturing Federation; Grenson Shoes Ltd; Joe's Shoe Repair (Shoes); Norelco Consumer Products; Philips Domestic Appliances and Personal Care (Shavers and razors); Distinctive Book Binders; The Folio Society; RS Book Binders (Books);

The Pentax Co. (Camera); Canterbury Bears Ltd; Pamela Thomas (Teddy bear); American Lighting Co.; F E Murdin, Decorative Lighting Association; Habitat (Lamp); Stihl (Chainsaw); Chingford Reproductions Ltd; Henredon (Chair); Braun Inc. (Food processor); Allens Typewriters Ltd; American Business Machines; W A Beeching; G F Currill (Typewriter); Carlton UK Ltd; US Leather & Luggage Co. (Suitcase); Black & Decker Inc.; Dualit Ltd (Toaster); Fulton Umbrellas Ltd; Sol Schaverien & Sons Ltd; Zip Jack Umbrellas (Umbrellas); J B Dove; Elmco; Toro Wheelhorse UK Ltd (Lawnmower); W&H Gidden Ltd; Miller Harness Co. (Saddle); European Gift & Houseware; Fairfax Engineering Ltd; Pavoni SPA (Espresso machine); Burberry's of London; London Town Corporation (Trench coat); Emey's Bicycles; F W Evans Cycles Ltd; Trek UK Ltd (Bicycle).

Additional design assistance:
Sandra Archer, Paul Calver, Simone End, Nicki Liddiard

Additional editorial assistance:
Susan Bosanko, Deirdre Clark, Edwina Johnson, Gail Lawther, Christine Murdock

Index:
Elaine Mills